CITIES IN THE SUBURBS

CITIES

IN THE SUBURBS

Humphrey Carver

UNIVERSITY OF TORONTO PRESS

ISBN 0-8020-1218-3 (cloth), ISBN 0-8020-6049-8 (paper)

The author wishes to acknowledge the generous support of
Central Mortgage and Housing Corporation, without
which the preparation of this book would not
have been possible.

Twelve Drawings by ZOLTAN KISS

CONTENTS

ILLUSTRATIONS

Drawings
by Zoltan Kiss

Plates

CREDITS. (1) Business and Industrial Photographers Ltd.; (2, 4) Public Archives of Canada; (3) Toronto Transit Commission; (5, 8, 10) Hunting Survey Corporation Ltd.; (6) The Photographic Survey Corporation Ltd.; (7, 28, 35, 39–42, 45) Central Mortgage and Housing Corporation; (9, 11, 18, 19) National Film Board of Canada; (12) Art Gallery of Toronto; (13, 26) National Gallery of Canada; (14) Royal Ontario Museum; (15) Canadian Government Travel Bureau, Ottawa; (16) N. Slater; (17, 25) Neil Newton; (20) Panda Photography; (21) Department of Extension, University of British Columbia; (22, 23) Nova Scotia Film Bureau; (24) Henry Kalen; (27, 29, 31, 32, 33, 38, 43) Max Fleet; (30, 34) Bill Lingard; (36) John Fulker; (37) National Capital Commission; (44) Artona Studios.

CITIES IN THE SUBURBS

TRANSFORMATION
AND DISTRESS

1. Cities in the Suburbs

EVERYONE LIKES TO LIVE in the suburbs. Everyone pokes fun at the suburbs. That's fair enough. Everyone respects those who made the suburbs.
Everyone despises the suburbs. Everyone's friends live in the suburbs.
Everyone hates the kind of people who live in the suburbs. Everyone
wants bigger and better suburbs. Everyone thinks there is just too much
suburbs. You and I live in the suburbs—it's lovely to have a nice home
in the suburbs. The whole idea of the suburbs fills us with dismay,
alarm, and frustration. Almost everyone's business is dedicated to
making life in the suburbs more and more and more enjoyable. The
suburbs are a crashing bore and desolating disappointment. The suburbs
are exactly what we asked for. The suburbs are exactly what we've got.

The suburbs evoke confusing and contradictory sentiments, accusa-
tions and rebuttals, affirmations and recantations. Most of the things
that are said against the suburbs are elusive and unspecific and usually
in the language of caricature. Scatteration. Scrambled eggs. An architectural tundra. "There is no there there," said Gertrude Stein. "An aim-
lessness, a pervasive low-keyed unpleasure which cannot be described
in terms of traditional sorrows" is noted by David Riesman.

These protestations are stirred by three emotions: a sense of guilt, a feeling of alarm, and a presentiment of some bleak inadequacy in our suburban ideals. North American civilization has committed itself to enormous confidence in the whole idea of owning a home in the suburbs; we invite the world to judge us by what we have achieved in this expression of family and freedom and possession. And yet we have to admit that though our motives are not regretted and our opportunities have been privileged, the results are only middling fair—and sometimes terrible. We have a sense of guilt because we have had the opportunity to build great cities in a way of our own choosing (for we are our own masters) but we have settled for compromises and not really cared enough. True, here and there is to be found a touch of beauty and imagination in the suburbs; but this is rare. With most of what we have built we are frankly bored.

We have feelings of alarm and urgency because everything points to an immense growth of cities during the coming decades and there is no assurance that the next few square miles of suburbs will be any better than the last. If all we have is bad, more is going to be worse. Even if immigration comes to a stop we shall still be faced with an enormous task in housing our Canadian-born population. The host of children born in the 1950's will reach marriageable age in the 1970's. They are almost twice as many as the children born in the depression decade of the 1930's who are now buying suburban homes. The most reliable forecasters have predicted that in the next twenty-five years the populations of our cities will double. How are we going to house all these people? Do we have to change our whole picture of the suburbs as a quiet retreat from the crowded city? We begin to perceive that this thing we call "the suburbs" is in truth a new kind of city: Cities in the Suburbs. The energies and inventiveness of North Americans and our attitudes to the distribution of wealth have revolutionized the very nature of cities. We have let loose powerful forces that are spreading cities in a flood over farms and forests. We marvel at the vitality and ferocious appetite of these forces, as bulldozers claw into the green acres to make new suburbs. But in the wonder there is also a sense of alarm. Is suburban growth a galloping horse out of control without destination and purpose? Are we masters of our destiny or are we being taken for a ride?

We have a nagging sense of guilt in not having made the most of our opportunities. We are alarmed at what lies ahead. And we are frustrated because we possess no clear image of what we should be striving to accomplish.

People have been living in cities for a long time and the task of city building has been the vocation of a great many professional people:

architects, engineers, town planners, and public administrators. One might well have expected that there would have emerged some fairly clear ideas about the kind of physical environment that would best serve the purposes of city people, both collectively and individually. The public might well imagine that the intellectual elite of the city-building professions had been carefully collecting and checking evidence on the relationship between urban forms and human objectives and formulating worth-while goals. But, as two distinguished authorities on town planning have recently pointed out, such an expectation "would bring a wry smile to the face of anyone familiar with the actual state of the theory of the physical environment." Professors Kevin Lynch and Lloyd Rodwin, working at Harvard and M.I.T., observe that there has been no systematic evaluation of the whole range of urban forms in relation to human objectives. They point out that there has been much protestation about the purposes of city planning, but the decisions actually made for shaping the growth of cities usually have little connection with these declared objectives. There has been "only the most nebulous connection between act and protestation." The concept of the suburbanized city is still at a primitive stage.

Though Canadians share this perplexity with Americans, our situation is a little different. Some of our cities are ancient, honourable, and of substantial size, but we have only just started to play in the big league as an urban nation. Hitherto we have been able to look with some detachment at the big cities of the world, sometimes wistfully eying their glamour and culture, but more often being grateful that we inhabit a land of seemingly infinite open spaces without their congestion and claustrophobia.

In this phase of our history we now start on our first essays in the art of building big cities. We approach this task of expressing ourselves as an urban people with a fairly clean canvas. We do not inherit the massive confusion and ugliness that accompanied the first wave of industrialization in European and American cities, in the age of coal-fired factories and grimy tenements. Projected straight into the age of clean fuels, cellophane packaging, and a car with almost every bungalow, we have nothing to escape but our own inadequacy. And, for the first time in our history, most of the coming generation of city householders will be people who were themselves born and brought up in cities, either in Canada or in another country. The crowds and close associations of city life are familiar to them; to the task of city building they will not bring personal memories of life on the farm and in the country. Up to now the growth of our cities has come largely by migration from rural areas; only 40 per cent of Canadians who are now more than sixty years old were born in towns, and these were mostly small towns. But, henceforth, the source of city population will be very different; 60 per cent of all Canadians born in the 1940's have grown up in towns, most of them in cities with more than 100,000 population. And there has been a remarkable change in the nature of that other large source of our population, the immigrants. After the First World War, in the 1920's, more than half of all immigrants were on their way to work on farms. But during the 1950's only 10 per cent came to do agricultural work and the great majority were city people with city skills. From many lands they have brought with them memories of city life. They have not come to see a repetition of the confusion and errors of an earlier industrial revolution but in expectation of finding some new enjoyment of city life. What kind of city should we, and they, try to build?

Our frustrations, indecisions, and uncertainties in trying to answer this question are not just fancy. We are entering the unknown. No civilization before us has ever had to deal with this new kind of city, which sprawls and spreads so widely over the landscape, the city disguised as Suburbia. There are no precedents to follow, no models to be looked at. Kilroy was not here before. North Americans are once again pioneers on a new frontier. We have to make plans while time and a surging population press hard upon us. It is the next move in the succession of "big leaps forward" that have been the pattern of Canadian history. Each frontier break-through has made its own characteristic mark of settlement on the land. First there was the French possession of the St. Lawrence with its water-front communications and the spire of each parish church visible across the fields and the water, as a sign of authority and friendship in a lonely country; this still stands as perhaps the most successful Canadian expression of a community. Then there was the coming of the Loyalists, clustering in friendly informality on the tidal rocks of the maritime shore or chopping their way into the forests of Ontario to establish the business-like solid little King Streets and Queen Streets of their market-towns. Then, in the first quarter of this century, the great flood-tide of all races poured out onto the prairies and made the spreading western cities, with their wide streets under the arching sky. And now we break through another frontier of population settlement, out into the suburbs.

We should begin with an appreciation of the recent events that have caused the previous forms of city to be succeeded by the new kind of decentralized suburban city. The meaning of this transformation has been captured in that brilliant cliché "the Exploding Metropolis," whose author, Mr. W. H. Whyte, Jr., we have to thank for that other invaluable addition to the English idiom: "the Organization Man." It is true that the surface of the suburbs is scattered with the fall-out of an explosion. The analogy is a useful one in showing that many of the bits and pieces and functions of a city that used to be found at its centre are now spread around its circumference. There are statistics to show this change in the location of a city's functions. Most evident has been the shift of retail trade from central business districts to suburban areas. A recent survey of thirteen major American cities by Mr. Raymond Vernon (see his study *The Changing Economic Functions of the Central City*) revealed that in seven of these cities the central business district had suffered "not only a relative decline in retail sales but an absolute decline as well, a decline all the more remarkable because it occurred during a period when retail sales in the nation were growing prodigiously."

But the analogy of an explosion is not strictly accurate in its suggestion that a single dramatic event left an empty crater at the centre of the city. Quite to the contrary, the centres of all our big cities have a profile even more convex than before. The central city may have ejected some of its functions and thrown them out into the suburbs, but in the economic geography of the big city the strategic centre has become even firmer, more concentrated, and more valuable. Here is the watch-tower, the high point, the panopticon, the headquarters from which the working affairs of the great sprawling city are directed. A new generation of princely bureaucrats, the business executives, have inherited the throne at the centre of the city, and there they sit aloft in their towering palaces.

The directorial functions of the city centre have certainly survived the explosion, and with the enlargement of the whole urban region they will undoubtedly grow and multiply. But it is also true that many things that used to draw people to the centre of the city are no longer there. It is the core of the city, but is it any longer the heart of the city?

The explosion analogy is also not strictly accurate in the suggestion that the suburbs appeared out of a sudden cataclysm. But it is perhaps true that, like refugees from a disaster, those who took flight to the suburbs had no particular plan of what to do on arrival in the new territory. The target was Open Space, without any more clearly defined objective. Of course, this quest for open space had been gathering its explosive force ever since men and women left behind the open horizon of the farm and found themselves crowded into city streets. People did not come to live close together in cities because they liked living close together but because they wanted the money that city jobs promised. From the outset, the opportunity to avoid living close together has been the highest privilege conferred by success in the city. Country estates and summer camps, ranch houses and ranch wagons, tweeds and trees on the lawn—these are symbols of man's constant desire for separation and independence from the crowd. So it was inevitable that when industry had been able to provide its workers with the material necessities of life, this release from concentration in the city would be the final benefit bestowed. The universal possession of a family car and a separate family home is the ultimate privilege conferred by membership in our kind of industrial democracy. So the urban migrants, like the westward pioneers before them, have been heading out of town to find cheap land. This had been going on for a long time before the present explosion of population gave this migration its spectacular proportions.

Looking back to an earlier stage in the evolution of the suburbs, we can observe some simple, practical virtues in the previous city that was made by street-cars. Most of us grew up familiar with the long strip of store fronts lining the street-car route. Out from the downtown centre the cars plunged along, stopping every few blocks to put passengers down near home. This route was the spinal column of each suburban extension, the whole city having an attenuated plan, its long fingers stretching out into the countryside. The street-cars precipitated the first suburbs and these long, straight streets were warm and welcoming channels of light along which we travelled familiar journeys. It was a world of small businesses, not supermarkets, and we got to know the shopkeepers and struck up personal acquaintances that made us feel part of a neighbourhood. If we moved away we would sometimes return to visit them and report how the children had grown. As each long finger stretched out from the centre of town it could be measured off like a scale of the years. This is where the street-cars had reached when the First War started. This is where the string of shops had reached when the veterans built their homes and won themselves a place in the booming 1920's. This is where the town was literally stopped in its tracks through the depression years. This is where the children grew up.

The street-car had made a workable, simple, homely design for a city. The shops and churches and restaurants and drugstores and movies strung out along the route formed a kind of community "strip" rather than a community "centre." This spinal cord of community services was easily accessible on foot from the blocks of houses behind. A monotonous form of city, perhaps, but compact and economical, with a visible continuity of history. And besides playing its historic role in setting out the first shape of the suburbs, the street-car is also responsible for the central part of the city as we know it. Without the street-car to gather

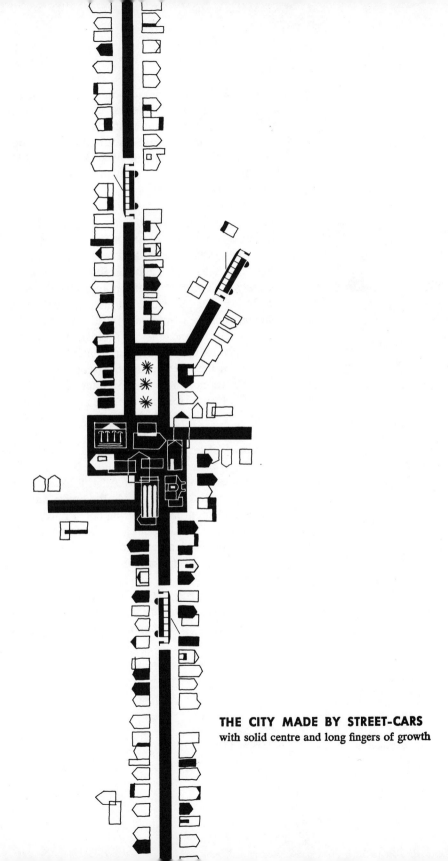

THE CITY MADE BY STREET-CARS
with solid centre and long fingers of growth

up thousands of pedestrians and deposit them at a single focal centre, much of the familiar aspect of Downtown would not exist: the big department stores, the many-storeyed office buildings, the busy elevators, the solid chunk of real estate. If this was the city of "The Danforth" it was also the city of Eaton's and Simpson's.

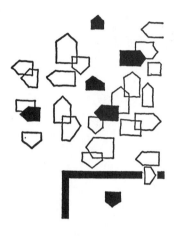

The mass-transit city had a characteristic pattern to it: a long stretching-out where people were carried on iron wheels, and a compactness of the downtown centre where they were carried on their own feet. This taut, rational, engineering pattern was blown to pieces by a technological and a social revolution. By 1930 the automobile was a neat, efficient vehicle comparable with the "compact" cars of 1961, and the technological revolution was ready to project the suburbanite out to the horizon far beyond the last street-car loop. At this point the economic depression intervened and, by a strange turn of fortune, brought about the social revolution without which the automobile could not have delivered its passengers to the distant suburbs. Out of the depression was born the system of government aid to families buying suburban homes. Without "N.H.A." in Canada and "F.H.A." in the United States the entire automobile-carried suburban scattering could hardly have taken place. On the secure economic foundation provided by government housing legislation the vast suburban house-building industry has been erected.

Government support for housing is an essential part of the whole welfare apparatus of the modern state. Whether the support takes the form of

THE SUBURBS BREAK LOOSE
scattered by the mobility of cars and trucks

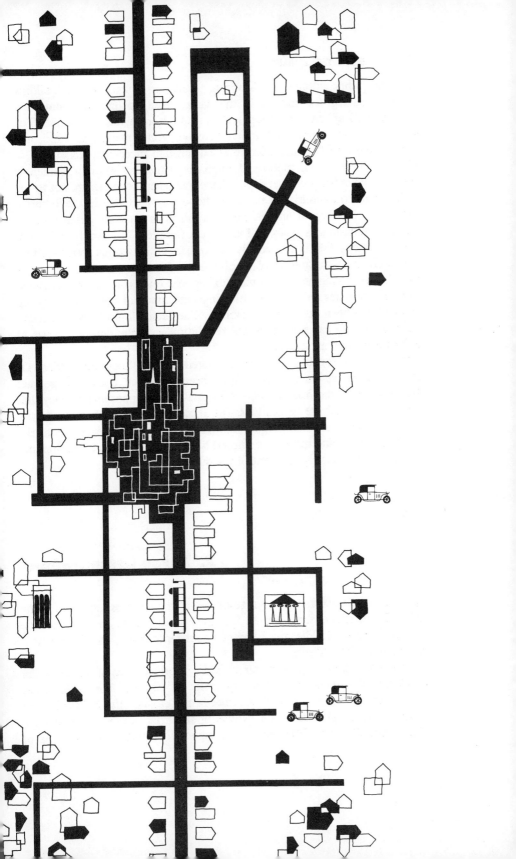

lending public money, of insuring mortgage loans, or of building public housing the motive is the same, even though the immediate receivers of aid may be people at very different levels of income. The first version of Canada's National Housing Act appeared in 1935, and it has been modified and supplemented through successive Acts in 1938, 1944, and 1954. The mood and emphasis of the first Act have somehow clung to its subsequent versions. There has been a dedication, not to the building of communities or neighbourhoods or new Cities in the Suburbs, but to the building of houses. Perhaps this is because the compassion of welfare programmes tends to focus upon families. The family is the one unit of society that is universally revered, in all languages spoken within our society: in the oratory of a politician to his constituents; in the commercialized sentiments of merchandising and real estate; in the accepted texts of churches and schools. Blessings and material possessions and all things have been added unto families. The technological revolution put the family in a car and the social revolution gave the family a house in the suburbs and all it contains.

These two revolutions have scattered and disintegrated cities. Of course, immense benefits have thus been bestowed upon city people; they have won the freedom and individuality and space and privacy that were the aims of the revolutions. But these benefits have been bestowed at the expense of other noble qualities of life, which used to be at the hearts of cities and are now scattered like dust, lost in the confusion and monotony and disappointment of the suburbs.

2. Three Lamentations

THOUGH THE COMPLAINTS AND SORROWS of the suburbs appear in many different versions, they can be grouped under three main titles: the Lament about Muddle, the Lament about Uniformity, and the Lament about What Isn't There.

You don't have to go very far to find a good example of the suburban city's muddle and confusion. Not five minutes' distance from where these words are written is a suburban street in the capital city of Canada that displays the tangled confusion typical of suburbia. It does not flatter the distinguished Prime Minister whose name it bears. Along one side of the street, with its counterpart on the other, in a distance of just one mile, are these buildings with a few empty lots interspersed:

two gas stations
a builders' supply plant
a house
a gas station
a house
a gas station
two small restaurants
a small apartment house
an old house
a delivery service garage
two houses
a gas station
a furniture removal warehouse
a florist's greenhouse
a house
a restaurant
a gas station
a grocery store
a barber shop
a restaurant
a large high school
a house
an elementary school
six houses
a licensed hotel

Most of this ill-assorted collection has arrived within the last ten years, an odd commentary on a city in which, at the same time, millions of dollars have been spent to make the national capital a place of beauty and reason.

It is true, of course, that cities always have rough edges while they are settling into shape. The miscellaneous raw material of cities has always been scattered at random along the Main Streets of North America, like the jetsam washed up on a tidal beach. The newer the city the more "raw" the material; for, as time passes, the stuff cities are made of tends to drift into a pattern. Shops doing the same kind of business tend to congregate. Professional people cluster together. What is relevant and compatible comes together; what is alien pulls apart. So a city, moulded in time by custom, convenience, and economics, gradually assumes an internal consistency which reveals the nature of its life and work. This is a quality that may give enjoyment of an aesthetic kind, just as does a mature work of art.

The incompatible material thrown up nowadays along our main arteries has a particularly crude and raw appearance, for two reasons. It is scattered in a much looser and more straggling fashion as the whole space-time dimension of cities has been stretched out. A promiscuous use of land is made possible by cars and trucks; the hunt-and-peck form of real estate development is encouraged by a vehicle that can bypass, leap-frog, and skip the intervening spaces to reach the cheaper land. Furthermore, the raw material itself that is spewed out by cities has become more and more diverse and miscellaneous. The suburban landscape has become cluttered with an ever larger miscellany of buildings and mechanical apparatus as city life has multiplied our possessions and occupations and interests. We need only to open the yellow pages of a city telephone directory to contemplate the diversity of professions, trades, and services that are nourished by a large city, each requiring some specialized equipment and accommodation: morticians, mortgages, motels, and masseurs; market researchers, marriage counsellors, and music arrangers; machine tools, mobile homes, and monument makers. No item in this paraphernalia of the modern city is inherently offensive or ugly—if smelly and noisy industries have been weeded out and isolated. Gas stations and common roadside restaurants should give colour and gaiety to the scene, and be a pleasure to look at and to use. We have not yet learned to appreciate the new and strangely beautiful shapes devised by engineers in electronics and chemistry, the spheres and volutes and spirals, the architecture of power and speed. The artefacts of the modern city offer ever fresh aesthetic qualities. The novelty and diversity of these forms are not in themselves offensive, but the contradictions in the way they are placed can be extremely disturbing.

This first Lament, about muddle and confusion, is a legitimate complaint. Few will defend the horror of Montreal's Decarie Boulevard, the brutality of Toronto's upper Avenue Road, Winnipeg's Pembina Highway, and the leagues of dreary sprawl between Vancouver and New Westminster. Here essential services of the city, thrown out into the suburbs by the explosive forces of urban growth, have been left in a disorganized assortment. There has been a failure to sort out the raw material, arrange it in compatible groups, and put these groups in the right places—either in the living areas or in the working areas of the suburban city. Can we afford to wait for this to happen gradually, through the natural processes of urban economics?

The second Lament, the complaint about Uniformity, raises a much more intractable problem because it is a complaint about the very thing that everyone claims to want. We staged a technological and social revolution, we got cars and home-financing, so that everyone could take the long road out to the suburbs. This was to be a way of life offering the greatest opportunity for the free expression of the individual. And here at the end of the road is the modern suburb with its stereotyped houses and the threat of stereotyped behaviour. It turns out that life in the suburbs is not such a privilege after all. Almost everyone else lives there too. There are more of us all the time and there are fewer differences between us. The less privileged families live in 1,000 sq. ft. bungalows, the majority live in 1,200 sq. ft. houses, and the really privileged live in 1,400 sq. ft. Only 200 square feet and a difference of a few inches in the lengths of our cars separate the sheep from the goats. The flight to the suburbs has taken us to a monotonous, standardized environment where everyone has much the same amount of money to do much the same things in the same ways. This is the complaint.

Long before the present generation of sociologists and psychologists had started to probe the behaviour of the suburbs, diagnosing the traumatic effect of living next door to someone rather like yourself, this difficulty had been foreseen. John Stuart Mill, in his famous essay on *Liberty* written just a century ago, commented in these words upon the frightening drift towards collective mediocrity:

Formerly, different ranks, different neighbourhoods, different trades and professions, lived in what might be called different worlds; at present to a great degree in the same. Comparatively speaking, they now read the same things, listen to the same things, see the same things, go to the same places, have their hopes and fears directed to the same objects, have the same rights and liberties, and the same means of asserting them. Great as are the differences of position which remain, they are nothing to those which have ceased. And the assimilation is still proceeding. All the political changes of the age promote it, since they all tend to raise the low and to lower the high. Every extension of education promotes it, because education brings people under common influences, and gives them access to the general stock of facts and sentiments. Improvement in the means of communication promotes it, by bringing the inhabitants of distant places into personal contact, and keeping up a rapid flow of changes of residence between one place and another.

The suburbs are the ultimate destination of all the factory-made building-materials and furniture, all the nationally advertised consumer goods, and all the precast ideas that issue from the diverse batteries of industry and commerce and social institutions. This is where the standardized product is finally delivered and where it stays: our common possessions made alike so that they will fit on the outside and on the inside of every suburban home and every suburbanite's mind and body. They are alike so that everyone can receive them—and almost everyone does.

The economics of house-building are, of course, heavily loaded in favour of standardization both in the original construction and for subsequent maintenance. Interchangeability of materials and of parts is an insurance against high costs of replacement. So the materials and the dimensions and the equipment of house-building must more and more bear the imprint of standardized industrial production, like the interchangeable replacements of a car.

Interchangeability is inherent also in the economics of the market for buying and selling houses. The whole house must, interchangeably, fit each new family household that will enter it on an average five-year turnover. The more standardized and the less specialized the house is, the more easily will it fit the changing requirements through its years of service to the community. So a heavy hand of conventionality has been laid upon the design of houses by mortgage companies and real estate investors. The house must be built around approximations and compromises. Statistically, three bedrooms give an approximate fit for the widest range of family sizes and compositions. The interior plan must approximate to the widest range of family living habits: there must be a place to eat in the kitchen but there must also be a dining space opening off both kitchen and living-room so that there is no commitment to either position. In its outward form the house must approximate to the "mean" of all varieties of taste for domestic architecture, neither too conservative nor too advanced—for who knows what are going to be the prejudices of the next occupant?

There are other items in the complaint about the uniformity of the suburbs. There is the complaint that zoning by-laws and subdivision practices and social prejudices have denied to family neighbourhoods every feature that might give variety, surprise, and contrast to the scene. No kind of building but a family house shall enter here. No apartment houses for young people or flats for old people. No corner store. No housing for those who are outside the privileged circle of home-owners. None who are too poor or too rich. Sterilized and inviolate under the protective shield of by-laws, the rows of small homes are immaculate in their uniformity, in their infinite repetition. How could this standardized material of the city be made into a work of art? However exquisite the tone, the insistent repetition of one note upon a single instrument is a form of torture. The small single house may be a pleasing and unassertive object, but in quantity it can be deadly. That is the complaint.

And then there is the bald and featureless landscape, scraped by the housing developer's bulldozer to remove all traces of nature. This violent pleasure in clearing a site has its origin in the pioneering past pictured in *Maria Chapdelaine*. The bulldozer is the modern version of the steaming horse, flinging himself against the traces as he takes the load of the settlers' stumping machine. "A short and desperate charge, a mad leap often arrested after a few feet as by the stroke of a giant fist; then the heavy steel blades would swing up anew, gleaming in the sun, while the horse took breath for a moment, awaiting with excited eye the word that would launch him forward again." The robust and manly vigour of the pioneer had its reward in the patch of cleared land "superbly bare, lying ready for the plough," a level champaign to be contemplated with "something of a mystic's rapture." So does the modern subdivider contemplate the land stripped of its offending trees and soil.

There are many verses to this Lament about Uniformity and some are more convincing than others. The case can be greatly exaggerated. In his spirited attack upon the dreadful influences of collective conformity Mr. W. H. Whyte, the heir to John Stuart Mill in the defence of our liberties, warns us to make a distinction between external similarities and what may lie beneath the surface. "We should never allow ourselves," he writes in *The Organisation Man*, "to be complacent about the external similarities." But we should not fail to recognize

that these similarities are in great part a consequence of making the benefits of our civilization available to more people. The monotonous regularity of ranch-type houses that can so easily appal us is not the product of an inner desire for uniformity so much as the fact that modular construction is a condition of moderate-cost housing. This kind of housing is no more or less a pressure for inner conformity than the rows of identical brownstones of the 1890's or, for that matter, the identical brick fronts of the 1700's.

The inevitable complaint about the monotony of suburbs exclusively composed of single-family houses, without provision for rental housing, or for young people and old people, raises a lot of questions. If there is to be "mixed" housing, how mixed should it be? What should be the richness of the mixture? In the language of the kitchen, should other ingredients be completely folded in and well stirred or should they remain as occasional incidents that retain their own distinctive flavour? On the map of the suburbs how frequently should those incidents occur; should there be a lot of small ones or a few large ones?

The answer hinges upon the needs of some households to be particularly close to stores, restaurants, public transportation, and recreation centres. The family household is a self-contained, independent operational unit, but the life of the apartment-dweller is incomplete and dependent. He must go out and get company and meals and make contact with the world around him. The placing of apartments and flats in the suburbs is therefore directly connected with the placing of community services. We have already noted that the metropolitan explosion has scattered many of these services along the main arteries of the suburbs. In just the same way apartment buildings are scattered at random in the suburbs, separated and dissociated. We have to bring together again these scattered fragments of the city and build them into new kinds of Cities in the Suburbs.

This brings us to the final lament that completes the triad: the Lament about What Isn't There, the expression of a shadowy intuition that Something is Missing. This lament is often cast in the abstract and emotional language of frustration. "There's no There there." People say there's "nothing to identify with"—whatever that may mean. The suburbs are just more of the same thing. Middle distances and middle incomes and middling results. No destination and nothing unexpected around the corner. Nothing very big and nothing very beautiful. The shopping centre's the most pronounced place; you've been there before and you come back bearing the same brown paper bag, for you're a consumer, average and typical. It's a relief to go downtown because it's large enough to lose yourself in. There are big buildings and even some beautiful buildings and you can look up and see the sky behind their summits. There are long distances and short distances as well as middle distances. They say downtown is now a place for the very rich and the very poor, a place of extremes, of excellence and of tragedy. In the open landscape of the countryside there are also great contrasts. You can see a long way and place yourself under the arch of the firmament. And on the ground are small things like flowers and pebbles. But in the suburbs there are no extremes.

The search for what is missing is a corollary of the other two laments. The word Confusion suggests that there is a lack of any system, method, or rationale; there is no apparent relationship of one thing to another—there is just chaos. The word Uniformity (or Monotony) is akin, suggesting that there is no system of variations, hierarchies, degrees. Everything is alike so the relationship between one thing and another has no substance. There are no proportions, no contrasts, and no harmonies. Confusion and Monotony are terms to be used in the criticism of cities in much the same way as they are used in literary criticism and in other kinds of appreciation. One may ask what is the plot of the story or what is the theme of the painting? So do we inquire: What is missing in the suburban city that makes it so chaotic and so monotonous? Where is the plot, the theme, the climax? What does it all lead up to?

Everything used to lead to the centre of the big city. But since the dispersal of the suburbs the centre of the city has not had the same significance. The suburbs are detached. Now there must be a new theme to the story, a new order and arrangement for a new kind of suburbanized city.

In the composition of cities, two qualities give shape and definition. One is the quality of order or system in the arrangement of the parts within the whole, in the manner of chapters within a book or movements within a symphony. The other is an intrinsic quality of the townscape and the landscape that gives character to a town, as poetry and painting receive an unmistakable individuality from the hand of an artist. For this latter quality there is no accepted word and, for purposes of this discussion, it will be called "inscape."

What is order and system in a city? We have already noted that the suburbs built by the street-car had a linear or strip system. All the community's services were stretched out along the line. At the principal intersections where the cars stopped, the services with the highest market priority placed themselves at the four corners; they might be banks, drugstores, or restaurants. Lower-priority services took their positions farther from the car-stop, the quieter institutions gravitating towards the less frequented stretches along the route. Immediately behind the two service frontages of the street-car route residential land was intensely developed, thinning out at greater distances from this spinal strip. The city made by street-cars embraced a price system, a transport system, a social system, and a design system.

Can we catch a glimpse of a new kind of suburban system that might bring order out of the chaos and monotony of today's suburbs, a successor to that last true urban system built by the street-car?

System has to do with the mechanical arrangement of the city. "Inscape" has to do with its poetry. To a certain extent cities can be explained in engineering terms but there are other aspects of city character that cannot be given such a mechanical explanation. Men take the materials of the earth's surface, the minerals and metals, the woods and growing plants, and out of these they build around themselves the wondrous form of a city. The places in cities which captivate our interest and remain in our memories appear sometimes to have happened almost by accident; sometimes they are places that have been consciously contrived. Whichever way they have occurred, these are the transcendent crowning glories of the countenance of any city, revealing its inner character. These expressive features may be in the landscape or in the townscape or, in certain places, even in the seascape. They are inherent to the particular city. They give it inscape.

In his interesting study *The Image of the City* Professor Kevin Lynch has developed the concept of "imageability" in reference to all kinds of features and characteristics of a city which make a strong impression on people's eyes and memories. These may be trivial and casual incidents in the townscape such as cracks in the pavement or a face at a window; they may be prominent buildings, or they may be the topographical differences between one district and another. The term "inscape" is used here in a more specific sense, in reference to the *genius loci* or *leit-motif* of a city which makes an emotional impact upon the heart and mind rather than just leaving a deposit upon the memory. This is something more than "imageability." The word "inscape" was used by the Jesuit poet Gerard Manley Hopkins to define the quality in anything in the natural world that moved him to poetry: the heaving surface of a rock, the bursting petals of a budding flower, the towering masses of clouds in the sky. The term "significant form" has some of the same sense when applied to a work of art, but does not fit the requirements of city description. The vocabulary of city planning unfortunately offers no word for the intrinsic and inherent qualities in those assemblies of buildings and landscapes that peculiarly command our attention and devotion.

You can identify these places in every city that you know. Water Street is the spine of St. John's in Newfoundland and on the harbour side is the long row of jetties; the masts of schooners bristle jauntily in the Atlantic air like an army of mediaeval lancers. What a scene around which to build a city! How different is Saint John, New Brunswick, with its solemn city Square raised on the height of land above the harbour, the steep ascent of King Street more formal than convenient—and beyond the Square the memories of past history in the old graveyard. Here is a strong elegiac statement. And what a contrast again with Fredericton, with its tall elms on the pastoral bank of the Saint John River, the Cathedral and the deanery, the portrait of Lord Glenelg in the antechamber to the Provincial Legislature, and Lord Beaverbrook's Gallery confronting the placid water. No other Canadian city has so captured the charm of a riverside site; strange, in a country of beautiful and historic rivers.

Quebec towns and villages of memorable inscape are legion. The houses packed close along the winding village street open up to form a gathering-place in front of the church. Or a grassy square with formal planting of trees frames a forecourt to the church facing across the river. Ste Anne de la Pérade seems like a stage set in a Victorian theatre and there is Ste Famille upon that Elysian island below Quebec. In a different mood is the landing place at Trois Rivières whose curious assortment of ancient and modern institutions tells the history of the nation. And there is that most remarkable of all viewing-places, the Dufferin Terrace in Quebec; here the native and the tourist meet on equal terms, the elderly make gossip, the young hold hands, and the children scamper, all sharing the same delight in the miraculous view over the comings and goings on the great river. Where else in North America do people simply stroll (or walk vigorously as if on the deck of a ship) for the pleasure of it and without embarrassment—alone, in couples, or by the dozen?

Our two largest cities offer an interesting contrast in their different emphasis on system and on inscape. In Montreal, the group of buildings, ancient and modern, that are grouped around Dominion Square and the new Place Ville Marie make a memorable and poetic composition that will surely always draw us to this heart of a great city. But Toronto, the home of the Canadian brand of Organization Man, is a master of system and has had the greatest difficulty in uncovering the poetry in its warm-hearted soul. In spite of strenuous efforts to give an air of distinction to University Avenue, which should have been the heart of the new city, this street has the emotional impact of two rows of stuffed shirts. One can try too hard.

Ottawa is fortunate in the possession of inscape. It has been blessed with a sympathetic topography and careful hands have been at work transforming what might otherwise have been just another business-like Ontario city. Rivers and canals and water scenery have provided many small-scale poetic compositions; the Bank Street bridge seen from the Driveway, the spire of Gatineau Point church seen from the Rockcliffe Lookout, the new campus of Carleton University—man has joined with nature in making these pleasures. In a capital city it is right that some of these scenes should have a wistful air of recollection and even a sadness; as we are reminded by Mackenzie King's gothic ruins so surprisingly set upon a Gatineau hill. There are emotions we miss in modern cities with their insistent hammering upon entertainment and achievement.

Some places in cities are impressive because of their associations with events and people. Whatever you may think of the architecture, however its appearance may change over the next thousand years, whether you have ever been there or not—eternally there is the corner of Portage and Main. Grandfathers, and uncles, and fathers-in-law from this spot took the first step into the West—50 miles, 500 miles, or 1,000 miles. And here for a younger generation was the moment of decision to go back East. All roads in Canada lead through Winnipeg's Portage and Main; it is more than just an example of local inscape.

There are, then, places in cities that have a strange power over us. This may be due to a supreme beauty of architecture or landscape that has been consciously contrived or it may be partly the inspiration of accident or it may come from a touching recollection of people and events. Surely the dissatisfactions with the suburbs are very much due to the absence of these memorable places that give meaning and expression to city life. This is the Lament about What Isn't There.

We are heirs to a long succession of city-dwellers who have known much the same yearnings, the same sorrows, and the same enjoyments as ourselves. Though social and technological revolutions have changed the shape and surface of the city, yet we ourselves have not changed as much as we sometimes think. So, before making proposals for the design of the contemporary suburbanized city, let us consider some of the themes and ideas about cities which we inherit from the past. The chapter that follows is an attempt to touch upon those that seem particularly relevant to our times.

TRADITIONS
AND IDEALS

1. Cities of Church and State

VISIONS OF MAN'S ULTIMATE DESTINY on earth, and indeed often in heaven, have usually taken shape around the image of a city. To build some kind of New Jerusalem or Celestial City has appeared to demand the most consummate artistry of which men are capable. Where hosts of people are gathered together to celebrate ultimate victory over the inhumanity and clumsiness of mankind there must surely be an ideal city. Prophetic revelation and Utopian gospel have, through the ages, presented visions of this imagined place. Though these visions have been blurred by the mists and disillusionments of history, yet the dream continues to recur in ever new forms. In fact we could hardly go on living in cities and working at the troubles they bring us, were it not for the dreams and idealizations tucked away somewhere in the backs of our minds.

It is impossible to contemplate a town or a city without seeing some kind of heart to it and some kind of boundary to it. All the imaginings and all the experience of succeeding generations in making cities have been concerned with the nature of what is in the middle and with the definition of the edges. What is the central purpose around which the city is gathered? How is the city related to the universe around it? These were the two ways of looking at ancient Babylon and they are still our preoccupation in dealing with the metropolitan city and its suburbia.

On hill-tops all over the world men first made refuges from their human enemies and from hairy beasts and from the unknown fears of the wilderness. People of the ancient world assembled on a fortress rock to defend themselves. They built walls around the summit and in their midst they built a shrine to their protecting deities. The Greeks called this rocky summit their Acropolis and when their battles had been fought and there was time to enjoy life, they devoted their highest talents to building at the centre of the hilltop city; the hewing of the Pentelic marble into the columns, floor, and roof of the Parthenon was a marvel of craftsmanship and in its sculptured figures of men and gods was presented the whole lusty drama of life. Boxed inside the massive temple walls were the mysteries, the oracles, and impenetrable secrets around which human destiny was believed to gravitate. The form of the early city was quite clearly defined by the walls that contained it and by the shrine at its centre.

The mediaeval city, as we can still see it in Europe and as its form has been handed down to us in legend and in picture, continued to have this sharp definition. Its battlemented walls clearly separated the open fields and forest from the closely packed houses sheltered inside. And, at the centre, the cathedral church raised its towering pinnacles into the sky. The emphasis on the central feature of the city had become even stronger; but the difference between temple and cathedral adds a new dimension to the concept of the city. The temple had been a sacred place to be looked at only from the outside. But the cathedral was a great hall of public assembly, inviting crowds to enter its cavernous doorways and meet under the great sheltering roof. It was a theatre, the stone vault echoing the chanting voices, its vast spaces mysteriously illuminated with sputtering candles and torches, the vault lifted high above the paved floor so that, in the sunlight, the immense windows displayed in pictures the stories of Christianity in torrents of flashing colour.

Through centuries of history this city appeared in many different shapes and styles but always with a single, clear focus. The city was a place of refuge, protected from the outside and centred upon a sacred place where each successive generation received its interpretation of the purposes and meaning of life and in turn passed on its own version of these mysteries. The mysteries of life were impenetrable and yet compelling; they could only be contemplated by shutting out the exterior world and addressing oneself to some kind of inspirational theology. In

THE ANCIENT AND MEDIAEVAL CITY
a fortified sanctuary

this mood ancient and mediaeval people were able to dedicate their city-making energies to the building of temples and great churches whose vast dimensions and lofty design still astonish us. All our mastery of scientific technique and understanding of human nature have not enabled us to reach again the perfection of the Greek Doric or the fourteenth-century Gothic, perhaps the most original and abstract creations of man's mind and hand.

But people are inquisitive and rebellious and are not willing to be satisfied by mysteries. Restless spirits caused that great change of direction in European life, the Renaissance and the Reformation. Life turned out to be much more provocative and complicated and understandable than had previously been supposed. Cities and ideas about living in cities no longer could be so simple and so obedient. It began to appear that a city must have many dimensions and splendours and could not be focused upon a single expression of theological mystery. The exterior world should not be shut out with walls but is part of the universe at man's command. The man of stubborn character, perverse independence, and lusty action began to break loose from the murky and legendary hosts of the Middle Ages. The portraits of Renaissance characters show us, not saints and abstractions of human qualities, but lively adventurers and rascals. So the town becomes the seat of merchants and princes and the market-place becomes a new focus of attention.

In the fifteenth century, for the first time, man began to see himself as a city-builder, consciously contriving a setting for himself, the actor. Instead of helplessly clinging to the citadel and crowding his houses under the shadow of the church, Renaissance man began to open up his cities in piazzas, squares, and vistas, setting the stage for his secular performance. The church still had its place of respect but the Prince's palace, the town houses of merchants, and the people's market square where bartering and haggling was to be done—these became the dominant elements in the city. So begins the great age of civic design that gave to Rome and Venice and Paris their many splendours. It is difficult for us to recapture the excitement of that dawning awareness of the Renaissance, the realization that people have authority to imprint their own desires and actions upon the world around them. Besides the tremendous quantity of buildings precipitated by the new vigour and mercantile enterprise of that period, there was for the first time an attempt to sketch out the form of the ideal city. This kind of speculative interest in the future was an essential part of the Renaissance mind, and had particular application to the building of cities. Artists and writers of the period were much concerned with the spatial organization of ideal cities.

THE CITY BECOMES A THEATRE
for the display of tastes and manners

The architects and engineers who designed the great civic compositions of Renaissance palaces and piazzas throughout Europe were in frequent professional communication with one another and were well aware of these idealizations. Leonardo da Vinci searched for knowledge of earth, air, fire, and water so that science and the creative arts might join in solving the problems of city life.

While it is true that a good deal of attention was given to superficial aspects of city design, yet in setting out the regular shapes of city squares and in arranging buildings on symmetrical vistas, the implications of social and sanitary engineering were not entirely forgotten. In *Selections from the Notebooks of Leonardo da Vinci* (Oxford University Press, 1952) are the following instructive suggestions:

> The high-level roads are six braccia higher than the low-level roads, and each road should be twenty braccia wide and have a fall of half a braccio from the edges to the centre. And in this centre at every braccio there should be an opening of the width of a finger one braccio long, through which rainwater may drain off into holes made on the lower-level roads. And on each side of this road there should be an arcade six braccia broad resting on columns.
>
> And if anyone wishes to go through the whole place by the high-level roads he will be able to use them for this purpose, and so also if anyone wishes to go by the low-level roads. The high-level roads are not to be used by wagons or like vehicles but are solely for the convenience of the gentle-folk. All carts and loads for the service and convenience of the common people should be confined to the low-level roads. One house has to turn its back on another, leaving the low-level road between them. The doors serve for the bringing in of provisions such as wood and wine, etc. The privies, stables and noisome places are emptied by underground passages situated at a distance of three hundred braccia from one arch to the next, each passage receiving light through openings in the street above, and at every arch there should be a spiral staircase. At the first turn there should be a door on entry into the privies, and this staircase should enable one to descend from the high-level to the low-level road.
>
> The high-level roads begin outside the gates at the height of six braccia. The site should be chosen near to the sea, or some large river, in order that the impurities of the city may be carried far away by water.

While Italy was deeply and magnificently involved in the artistic Renaissance, in the age of Leonardo, Raphael, and Michelangelo, the English were preoccupied with the religious and political problems of the Reformation. Even at this early stage English thinking about the problems of cities began to take its characteristic form, an intense concern for systems of government and social welfare. Sir Thomas More, an exact contemporary of Michelangelo, first published *Utopia* in 1518. Witty, urbane, and intellectual, More belongs in the tradition of English political satirists and iconoclasts; the pages of *Utopia* gave the same kind of entertainment and intellectual provocation that a later generation received from Bernard Shaw. The English have always been suspicious of fine architecture and grand city-planning that might obscure their puritanical concern for the individual, and some passages in this sixteenth-century satire foreshadow later events with curious perception.

The people of Utopia lived on a crescent-shaped island, about two hundred miles long and containing a large land-locked harbour between the two horns of the crescent. It is explained that about twelve hundred years earlier the people of this island had rescued a ship-wrecked crew of Romans and Egyptians, who stayed with them. The islanders proceeded to learn from this handful of unexpected guests all the useful arts they knew and "by the hints they gave them they themselves found out some of those arts which they could not fully explain." In the intervening twelve hundred years the islanders had made much better use of this information than had the rest of the world with all its wars and political muddles. On the island they had built fifty-four cities to a more or less standard design. "The nearest lie at least twenty-four miles' distance from one another, and the most remote are not so far distant but that a man can go on foot in one day from it to that which lies next it." The cities do not have more than six thousand people and there is no inclination to increase the size of each town, "for the people consider themselves rather as tenants than landlords." The buildings in the city "are so uniform that a whole side of a street looks like one house." The houses are described as having "great quantities of glass." The Utopians are sturdy socialists and have to eat in communal dining-rooms at the call of a trumpet. "No family may have less than ten and more than sixteen persons in it" and it is remarked by the author that "this rule is easily observed by removing some of the children of a more fruitful couple to any other family that does not abound so much in them." This standardization of family size is coupled with the arrangement that "at every ten years' end they shift their houses by lots." In the same spirit the sizes of cities were to be standardized by the export of surplus population to less-favoured communities.

The problems of suburbia are further anticipated by the following remarkable arrangement:

The jurisdiction of every city extends at least twenty miles, and, where the town lies wider, they have much more ground. . . . They have built, over all the country, farmhouses for husbandmen, which are well contrived, and furnished with all things necessary for country labour. Inhabitants are sent, by turns, from the cities to dwell in them; no country family has fewer than forty men and women in it, besides two slaves. . . . Every year twenty of this family come back to the town after they have stayed two years in the country, and in their room there are other twenty sent from the town, that they may learn country work from those that have been already one year in the country.

In the Utopian suburbs there is no toying with garden tractors and swimming pools. The townsman's thirst for open space is exploited to get some useful work out of him on the farm. And when he returns to the city he is well equipped to make his small garden fertile and productive.

Sir Thomas More, lawyer and public servant, was concerned with the organization of society rather than with the forms of cities. But, perhaps unwittingly, he here put his finger upon the issue that subsequent generations have been unable to resolve: how to reconcile town and country. How can the town be brought into the country? How can the country be brought into the town?

The Renaissance broke the unity of the city as a place of refuge and faith, and presented the great dilemma of city people in the choice between the benefits of corporate authority and individual freedom. This choice has been rather curiously associated in people's minds with the city and the country. The city is the place where you lose your identity in the crowd; the country is where you are isolated and alone with nature and, so it is commonly believed, therefore more free. To head for the open spaces, to the country, has always seemed to the city man to be the clearest gesture of independence. To turn towards the centre of the city, which represents power and dominance, has seemed to infer an acceptance of a higher order of authority. (Historians declare that this distinction between city and country is all an illusion. Were not liberty and commercialism born in the city, away from the restraints of the feudal system? Do not country folk continue to flock to the city, to seek freedom in choosing their careers and their companions?)

Here is an important divergence of thought and experience that flowed from the Renaissance. On the one hand is the essentially urban, civic, and classical tradition of formal manners in architecture and city planning. On the other hand is the romantic, frontier-seeking, cottage-in-the-suburbs impulse. The Townscape and the Landscape.

The power of monarchs and princes, the martial character of Napoleonic and dictatorial states, the authority of law and order—these have found their appropriate expression in the symmetry and rigidity of the classical styles of architecture and city planning. When North America sought to express the authority of the new democratic state it was difficult to avoid the use of these conventional expressions of power, however alien their earlier associations might be to American political philosophies. The design of Washington, first set out in 1798, fulfils the classical ideals of city building with its magnificent central axis tying

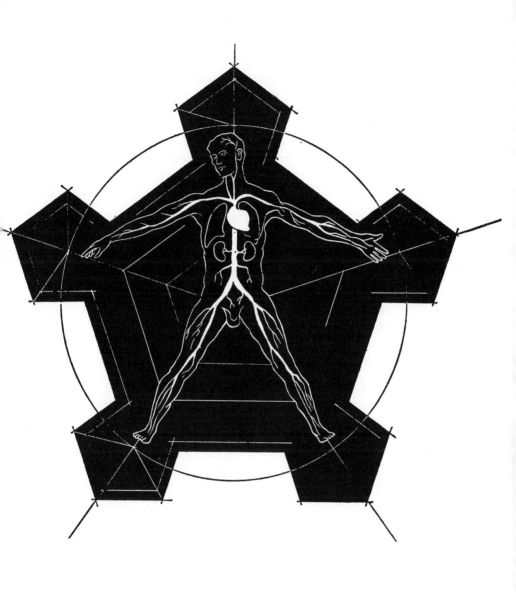

RENAISSANCE MAN IMPOSES HIS OWN DIMENSIONS AND IDEALS
upon the total form of the city

together Lincoln's Greek temple, George Washington's Egyptian obelisk, and the baroque dome of the Capitol. In Europe the Caesars, popes, and monarchies had attempted nothing on such a grand scale. In lesser situations, whenever it is the purpose to express the authority of the State and the presence of the organs of government and law, it is natural to seek inspiration from the same source. The modest legislative building in Charlottetown and the more flamboyant provincial parliaments in Winnipeg, Regina, and Edmonton have all adopted the formal pose.

Architectural compositions in the grand manner have provided a structural basis for the arrangement of cities, with the emphasis placed upon the institutions that are most deeply valued by society. For instance Sir Christopher Wren's master plan for the rebuilding of London after the great fire of 1666 proposed a series of formal positions for the city churches, with vistas and spaces to declare the full Renaissance dignity. In the present replanning of the central areas of Philadelphia there is a similar aim to restore the status of the old churches and public buildings and monuments, which had been lost in the later untidy growth of the city.

This formality at the heart of the city has to be reconciled with the other nature of city people that had its birth in the Renaissance and Reformation. In contrast with the unifying, concentrating, stately classic theme is the roving spirit, the striving for independence and individual enterprise without which there could not have appeared the eager, competitive Western society which has created the great regional city. So today's city in the suburbs must have a strong formality at the centre, but must not inhibit the expression of individuality and independence. The concentration of the city: the freedom of the country.

2. Town and Country

THE GARDEN CITY was invented to embrace the best of both worlds, the Town and the Country. For this brilliant compromise we are indebted to a quiet and thoughtful Englishman who had spent his youth in Chicago and in London and seen with his own eyes the first dreadful impact of industrialization. His penetrating insight into the problems awaiting our cities appeared in a famous work entitled *Garden Cities of Tomorrow*, published in 1898. Ebenezer Howard has been widely recognized as the first person to acquire and expound a comprehensive and systematic view of urban growth; but his reputation, like that of other Utopians, has suffered at the hands of those who have not troubled to read what he wrote.

In his book, in one sweeping vision, is the whole regional view of a great city's growth into the surrounding hinterland. The character of the city's centre, the problems of its growth, and the nature of the open countryside beyond are seen as related aspects of a single great task of regional city building. In the sixty years since the publication of Ebenezer Howard's work there has been no comparable revelation of the whole purpose and process of building great cities. Of course circumstances have changed immensely and, had he stood where we do in the unfolding industrial and social revolution, Howard's analysis would undoubtedly have led him to somewhat different conclusions. Meanwhile we still fumble with ideas that were largely given to us by this remarkable man—ideas of Greenbelts, Garden Cities and Satellite Towns, Land Assembly, Neighbourhood and Regional Planning. Since Howard made his original statement his ideas have been obscured by a certain amount of folk-lore, so perhaps we owe the author a second look at what he really proposed; this turns out to be more specific and constructive than the rather sentimental version of the Garden City doctrine with which his name has been associated.

Living and working in Chicago and in London in the eighties and nineties he saw the great migrations of factory workers piling into the central industrial districts, crowding into tenements and cottages. He saw their children multiply while the space they so badly needed was consumed by traffic and commerce. These migrants came from villages and farms, from places that are generally supposed to be the seat of all domestic virtues. Here in the congestion of the city they were degraded by gin and sin. Howard was a social reformer in the nineteenth-century tradition; he was not afraid to enliven his evangelism with purple passages from Dickens and Ruskin and he could himself turn an apt phrase: "The air is so vitiated that the fine buildings, like the sparrows, rapidly become covered with soot, and the very statues are in despair." His soul revolted against the familiar drab, gas-lit city and he was dedicated to stemming the tide of migration into the interiors of towns and to getting the working population back into the healthy countryside. There must be no more growth at the centre. Let city growth take the form of satellite towns thrown out into the green fields.

Howard's vision of a satellite Garden City was not at all the scene of widely spread homes and gardens that you might expect and he would undoubtedly have been revolted by our modern suburbia. By "garden city" he did not mean a city *of* gardens. He meant a city *in* a garden, a compactly built town surrounded by pastoral landscape. For each satellite town-in-a-garden he proposed the acquisition of 6,000 acres of which only 1,000 acres would be used for a town of 30,000 population, complete with its own industries, shops, and institutions. He proposed to tuck this population into 5,500 building lots averaging only 20 by 130 feet. It was indeed to be a *city* in a garden, not a glorified village. "The clean and busy streets within, the open country without," quotes Howard from Ruskin's *Sesame and Lilies*.

For the opening chapter of his book Howard drew a diagram of his ideal town. He was very careful to point out that this was no more than a schematic diagram; imagination would have to be used in translating its principles into the design for an actual site. Like so many Utopias, the Garden City is shown as a perfect circle. Radiating boulevards divide the town into six "wards" or, as we would now say, neighbour-hoods. At the very centre is a compact group of public buildings (town hall, theatre, library, etc.) enclosing a small park "laid out as a beauti-ful and well-watered garden." A larger park surrounds this civic com-position. The six residential "wards" are each planned to face inwards upon an interior girdle of open space 420 feet wide. Within this belt of parkland six four-acre sites are reserved for schools and their play-grounds and gardens, with other sites "reserved for churches of such denominations as the religious beliefs of the people may determine." In fact we have here the first prototype of the "neighbourhood super-block" later to be refined by Clarence Stein and Henry Wright at Radburn.

The factories and workshops of the town are strung out around its circumference (a prophecy of future industrial decentralization) and served by a ring railway. Thus the immediate barrier to the outward growth of the city is not the greenbelt but the industrial ring where workers look out upon productive farm and orchard land with a busy population of 2,000. Like other Utopians he espoused the union of factory worker and farm worker, hoping that they would bring a blessing upon one another by the proximity provided in his plan.

The passing of time has given an archaic quality to some of Howard's suggestions. Encircling the Garden City's central park was to be a con-tinuous glassy structure, which would combine the functions of shopping centre and enclosed Winter Garden. It is entitled the "Crystal Palace."

EBENEZER HOWARD'S MISSION
to build a constellation of satellite towns
in the green fields

There are overtones of the Victorian conservatory with its damp potted palms and of the pavilion on the pier at Brighton, with string orchestras and afternoon tea. This idyll of our grandfathers has lost its enchantment but the proposal demonstrates an intention that the residents of the town would look inward towards the focus of their social institutions. Though the plan embraces both town and country it hangs together as a centripetal community.

This elaborated sketch of a satellite city is largely a device on which to hang the main economic thesis that occupies the greater part of the book. Howard was compassionately and deeply concerned about the living conditions of the new industrial population crowding the centres of cities; he points out the immense costs that would be involved in giving them *in that location* the schools and living space and all the amenities of civilization that should be expected in a land of such industrial wealth. He quotes the fact that land for schools within central London had been costing £9,500 ($50,000) an acre and states that land for a Garden City out in the country could be bought at £40 ($200) an acre. Through the public acquisition of a 1,000-acre townsite he calculates that the total cost of all the land for private and public purposes could be reduced to the trivial figure of one shilling and one penny annually for each person in the 30,000 population. For all practical purposes the cost of land would be wiped out as long as the townsite remained the property of the community. Howard sums up in these words the two simple expedients by which his scheme would bring immense economic benefits to society:

First: by buying land *before* a new value is given to it by migration, the migrating people obtain a site at an extremely low figure, and secure the coming increment for themselves and those who come after them.

Second: by coming to a new site they do not have to pay large sums for old buildings, for compensation for disturbance and for heavy legal charges.

Howard's vision of *Tomorrow* (the title of his book in its first edition) had a clarity and originality that made an immediate appeal. He stuck to general principles and did not attempt to go into details that would quickly have become out of date; the very dryness of the social document has preserved it for posterity while a more lyrical form of expression would have faded with the passing fashions. By 1902, only four years after the first publication, the first Board of Directors of a company had been appointed to carry out the Garden City idea. Howard claimed that he had hit upon a plain, common-sense proposal which was "a leaf taken out of the book of each type of reformer." People of very different backgrounds and political persuasions found common ground here. A contemporary, C. B. Purdom (in *The Building of Satellite Towns*), noted that "the Socialist liked it because of its semi-municipal character, and at the beginning of the century Socialism on its practical side was strongly pro-municipal; the Conservative because it promised a way in which private enterprise could help to solve the housing question; the Liberal because it was a project of land reform." The Directors of "First Garden City Limited" got down to business quickly and only a year after organization had acquired a site of 3,800 acres for about £160,000 in a rural area of Hertfordshire, thirty-four miles from London. Letchworth was a small hamlet on the site and this became the name of the first Garden City. Through the decade up to the beginning of World War I the town grew steadily year by year till it had a population of 10,000. At this stage, immediately after World War I, also on the initiative of Ebenezer Howard, the sister community of Welwyn Garden City was started on another site in Hertfordshire only twenty-one miles from London.

Now, fifty years later, Letchworth is still largely owned by "The First Garden City Company Limited." Welwyn Garden City was acquired by the national government after World War II, to be further expanded as one of the eight new towns built by public development corporations outside London, to receive the overflow of industry and population. The greenbelt lands which were part of the original acquisitions have been incorporated in the larger belts of rural land now preserved from urban use through national planning policies. Thus Ebenezer Howard's imaginative ideas and two practical experiments have profoundly affected the history of city growth in Britain.

Any study of town planning is bound to treat the figure of Ebenezer Howard with awe, as if he were indeed one of the Prophets. For the stream of imaginative thought and experience which has flowed continuously from this fountain-head is still as fresh as ever after more than half a century. There has been an impressive fraternity of those who have dedicated themselves to these same objectives on both sides of the Atlantic; Sir Raymond Unwin and Sir Patrick Abercrombie in Britain, and Lewis Mumford and Clarence Stein in the United States, are only the most distinguished names in the company of those who have fought in this cause against the inertia of public opinion and government practice. From this source has flowed the stream of events that bore the fifteen New Towns of Britain built after World War II, certainly the most dramatic achievements of model town-building. This was the source, too, of Radburn and the American Greenbelt towns of the 1930's, still regarded as prototypes of good community-planning.

Whether the aim is to build an ideal city in the wilderness, like Kitimat, or to realize a realtor's dream in the suburbs—we keep on coming back again to Ebenezer Howard. But we never quite catch up with him.

From 1903 to 1906 the secretary of "First Garden City Limited" was the same Thomas Adams who came to Canada in 1914 as adviser to the federal government, to study problems of rural conservation and the settlement of the new immigrant populations. He drafted the first town-planning legislation in Canada, laid the foundation of a new profession of city planners, and carried out several housing projects, among them Lindenlea in Ottawa and the Hydrostone housing in Halifax on the scene of the great munitions' explosion described so graphically by Hugh MacLennan in *Barometer Rising*. Thomas Adams moved to New York City to direct the truly monumental series of studies of the city's regional plan carried out in the 1920's. Among these studies, perhaps the most lasting monument in the series, is Clarence Perry's now famous statement of "The Neighbourhood Unit." This was the first definitive description of a completely self-contained community within a surrounding urbanized territory, a community of about 5,000 people on an area of about 160 acres. Clarence Perry was not dealing with a politically idealistic situation; he accepted the stubborn reality that New York and other North American cities are going to grow by continuous accretion and not by throwing out satellite Garden Cities. He sought a workable form for this kind of local community development. The model plan was based on four general principles:

1. An elementary school should provide the focus of each neighbourhood, the school being designed for general community uses as well as for children. At a housing density of about ten families to the acre the school would be accessible to about one thousand children without any having to walk too far.

2. Interior streets of the neighbourhood should not be attractive to through-traffic but useful only for reaching the school, churches, and community park at the heart of the neighbourhood. Each neighbourhood unit would be separated from the surrounding city by the main traffic streets.

3. Shops and apartments should be at the outside corners of the neighbourhood area where the main intersections and heaviest traffic are found.

4. 10 per cent of the land should be reserved for parks and recreation.

Clarence Perry's version of the Neighbourhood Unit set within a continuous suburban district seems to us today a very mild kind of ambition. But it has to be seen in the context of the great real-estate boom of the twenties, which threatened to enclose every North American city from Edmonton to New York, from Toronto to Los Angeles, with an infinite rectangular gridiron of streets. Surely there could be some relationship between the organic pattern of a living community and the pattern of its streets and land forms? Though the point is now self-evident, its first statement by Perry is still contemporary because it took several decades to use up the gridiron lands inherited from the thirties and it was only in the fifties that it was generally possible to do "neighbourhood" planning on virgin territory.

Perry's Neighbourhood Unit was hopefully focused on the social institutions of school and church; traffic and commerce were banished to the exterior. Surrounded by the noise and cluttered streets of New York City, pressed on every side by the racket of commerce and the dark shadows of industry, this was a natural response. It was the mission of the Settlement House and working Christianity to retrieve family life from the kind of city conditions that had appalled Ebenezer Howard a third of a century earlier. The Neighbourhood Unit was offered as a protective measure for the working man's family rather than as a prescription for building finer cities.

Meanwhile, however, a more sophisticated idea had been maturing in the perceptive mind of Clarence Stein, an American architect who numbered among his friends Lewis Mumford, Stuart Chase, and other members of a congenial group who gathered in the name of the Regional Plan Association of America. Stein, known to a later generation of Canadians as the planner of Kitimat, visited England after World War I and was touched with the zeal of Ebenezer Howard's disciples who were advocating the building of One Hundred New Towns and were already at work on the second Garden City of Welwyn. But, as an American, he could not translate to his own country the spirit of the "city in a garden" without providing for the motor-car that had come to change our lives; henceforth any idealization of city living must take account of this new phenomenon, not simply banish it to the boundaries of the neighbourhood. The town of Radburn, designed in 1928 by Stein and his partner, Henry Wright the landscape architect, offered an entirely new way of living at peace with the automobile. In his introduction to Stein's *New Towns for America*, Lewis Mumford points out that the key to this puzzle was already available to Stein as a New Yorker, familiar with Frederick Olmsted's design for Central Park.

Olmsted's complete separation of pedestrian walks from vehicular and horseback traffic, by means of overpasses and underpasses, in Central Park, was certainly the major fore-runner of the Radburn plan. Unfortunately Olmsted himself never apparently grasped the general significance of this separation for modern planning, particularly on land whose contours offer different levels. But one can hardly doubt that Stein's daily walks through Central Park during this formative period encouraged him to hold to it tenaciously, once Radburn was built.

Radburn, in suburban New Jersey, is neither a complete satellite town nor a Garden City in the Ebenezer Howard sense (it is not surrounded by a rural greenbelt); the plan to build a community for 25,000 people was interrupted by the economic collapse of the thirties. But like a great sculptor's unfinished masterpiece that shows some of the unhewn rock-face, Radburn is a landmark in man's quest for a better way of living; this noble fragment even gains some dramatic effect from being tucked away in the back blocks of a New Jersey borough. The idea of the "Radburn Plan" has been received and copied, plagiarized, perverted, misunderstood, and misapplied all over North America and in many other parts of the world. It is a town turned outside-in, with houses turned around so that living and sleeping rooms face towards gardens and parks, with service rooms facing towards streets. It is a town in which roads and parks "fit together like the fingers of your right and left hands"; the park is the backbone of the neighbourhood, opening into the large spaces at the centre of each superblock and joining with a thread of space to the next park.

In his own story of his successive experiments in town design, in *New Towns for America,* Stein attributes the idea of "the house turned around" to his colleague Henry Wright and recalls Wright's own recollections: "In 1902, as an impressionable youth just out of architectural school at Waterford, Ireland, I passed through an archway in a blank house wall on the street, to a beautiful villa fronting upon spacious interior gardens. That archway was a passage to new ideas." From within the privacy of home the family looks out upon figures in the landscape; the garden is a place of social enjoyment, not a place shut away from view. This is the most ancient form of garden, the cool space of the Arab and Mediterranean house, cut off from the hot, dusty streets of the city.

3. Poetry and Polemics

TWO MEN OF GENIUS have given vivid expression to the choices that face twentieth-century city-builders. Le Corbusier, the European, and Frank

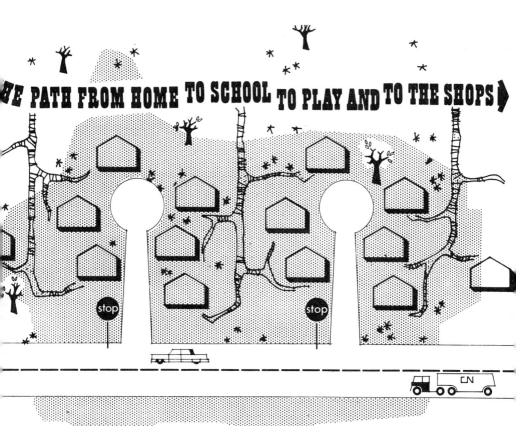

CLARENCE STEIN'S RADBURN PLAN
to separate people from vehicles

Lloyd Wright, the American, captured the imagination of the public and attached to themselves a dedicated following of architects and planners. They have had an enormous influence upon the look of the cities around us. The North American suburban bungalow would not look the way it does had it not been for Frank Lloyd Wright; the houses that he designed forty years ago, such as the Robie house in Chicago, were the prototypes of the "open plan" house which is now the accepted setting of suburban family life. The soaring slabs of office buildings and apartment blocks would not be as they are if it had not been for Le Corbusier's prophetic formulation of this structural shape forty years ago; in every urban centre in the world are buildings derived from his sketches for the United Nations headquarters in New York. The personalities of these two men are stamped indelibly upon the forms and manners of all our cities, and their influence reaches into every place where there are cities and suburbs.

Apart from their influence upon the actual surface appearance of cities these two men have been at the vortex of discussion about the shape of things to come. At a time when the stability of civilization has been disturbed by new social and political philosophies and by new comprehension of man's place in the physical universe, there had to be equally profound questionings about the forms of cities as expressions of man's place in society. Is the individual personality the most important focus of life, with all its possessive, perverse, and self-centred qualities? Or is the individual to be regarded as but a temporary member of a larger and more crowded continuity of people that is the real stuff of which cities are made? These are the questions that seem to be symbolized in the characteristic works of Le Corbusier and Wright. On the one hand is the massive concrete monolith, the "Unité d'Habitation" behind Marseilles, which expresses the solidarity and impersonality of congregated living. And on the other hand is "Broadacre City," in which the mid-western American emphasized the release of individuals in sprawling property ownership, each going his own way in his own fashion. On these two positions people tend to take sides in argument. Undoubtedly there is truth on both sides and the issue is not so much a matter of conflict as of complement.

Though Le Corbusier's influence and work in many parts of the world have made him an international figure, yet he remains essentially a European and more particularly a Parisian. His appreciation of the intensity of life in a great metropolitan city compelled him to pour scorn on the "family home," "the universal waste land of garden cities," and the "easy hypnosis of satellite towns." To build satellites around a great

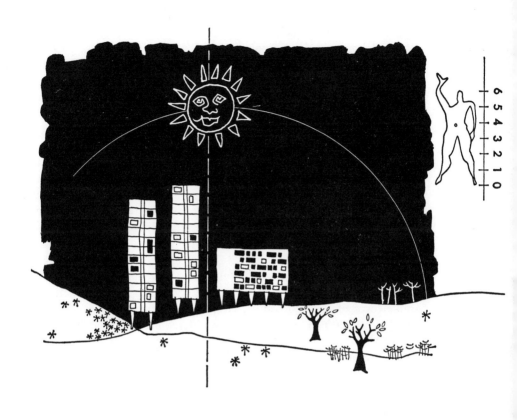

LE CORBUSIER'S SCULPTURAL CITY
vertical in space

city, he claimed, would not only drain off people from the metropolitan centre but would eventually pull to pieces the work-centre itself leaving the old city nothing but a strangled network of streets entirely unable to carry the assault of traffic rushing from one outlying point to another. "The ancient city is empty. It has become a void. The houses are deserted: the haunts of vagabonds. The abandoned buildings fall in weedy decay. They must needs be abolished," declares Le Corbusier in *The Home of Man*. The threat of dispersal of the great city into the ever extending spider's web of satellite towns made Le Corbusier the first proponent of a massive programme of urban renewal. The packed, narrow-corridor streets of the central city must be removed to open up wide green spaces as the setting for towering residential blocks exposed to the sun and the wind and embracing wide views of the sky. He shows that three million people could live in a green and radiant city of inner Paris with space left over, and so fulfil the destiny of the city as a great centre of thought and administration and commerce, housing its incomparable force of talented people. He points out that to house a population of 1,600,000 in garden cities would require eight satellite towns each with a diameter of 2¾ miles, but the same population could be housed in one vertical city of green spaces on a single area of 2¾ miles' diameter and "all around it an immense countryside will be freed; fields, meadows, forest. . . ." He compares the cost of putting 500 dwellings in a single high building with the cost of 500 single suburban houses. In the first case only 6 acres is required for the building, 3 linear miles of services, and 500 yards of roadway. For the same number of single houses 51 acres would be needed, 35 miles of services, and 3¾ miles of roads. A true satellite town, Le Corbusier argues, is not this instrument for the assassination of a great city but an industrial centre a hundred miles or more away from the metropolitan capital, where raw materials are processed. Here he does admit clusters of family houses, taking their place in parallel with the assembly line of industrial production. The small country village is also a cluster of houses, gathered around a centre of co-operative community services. A place for the family house is conceded where it is set amidst meadows and trees.

The impact of Le Corbusier upon the minds of his architectural contemporaries in the 1920's was not just that of an invigorating fresh wind on a sultry afternoon. It was a sensation: like the arrival of the first sputnik in the fifties. Suddenly an entirely new dimension of imagination was opened up. Until this moment the whole vocabulary and art of architecture and city planning had been an extension of the past. Styles of architecture had faded and been revived in cycles of taste. The

Garden City movement was frankly an escape from the big city as something monstrous and beyond comprehension; the streets and houses of the satellite town were to be comfortably small in scale, reminiscent of the picturesque mediaeval villages and the polite eighteenth-century small town. One could look back into the past for the things that seemed desirable, but the future was a blank. Then, suddenly, there burst upon the world an altogether new revelation of the big city as a bold and exhilarating place, a fitting challenge for the technical skills and healthy bodies of a new urban generation. The curtain was drawn aside to show a new age.

Not the least of Le Corbusier's gifts is his highly personal, ecstatic style of self-expression on paper. In a few liquid, scrawling doodles of the pen and a few exclamatory words he somehow managed to capture a fresh universe of city enjoyments. The sculptor, the painter, the writer, and the illustrator were joined in one. The big city was made alive and comprehensible. The world itself was seen as a globe upon which we turn, a mobile with the light of the sun falling upon its turning surface. We watch the behaviour of men as they come out into the sun and retreat into the shadows, their figures moving in the rhythm of day and night as the tilting of the earth causes the succession of the seasons. So in a few scribbled lines we see a great complex of skyscrapers standing out from the page in dreamy reality, their shadows cast on an infinite Bois de Boulogne.

Le Corbusier seized the problem of Town and Country and raised it out of the romantic and dainty scale of the suburban garden city. He dealt like a giant with the landscape of sky and sun and rolling hills. The family is not to be enclosed by small hedges and picket fences; it is lifted up and shown the horizon from the upper floors of the great city Habitation. The whole building is itself lifted from the ground on stilts so that the landscape goes rolling on right through and underneath. The hand of a giant is set also upon the materials of the building; the surface of the reinforced concrete is rough-hewn, the imprint of the planks showing like chisel marks on massive stone. The vigour of architectural shape and texture is, more than anything else, like the archaic Greek Doric of Sicily and the Aegean, the work of a sculptor touched with the strong colours of pure paint, the heroic abstract forms shining in space. To a world that had been chained to escapist romances in Gothic and Georgian and New England fashion, to regrets and nostalgias, this new architecture of the city had a pristine freshness to it that had not been felt since the Renaissance.

Here there is some common ground between the European and the mid-western American. Frank Lloyd Wright also engaged in vigorous manhandling of the materials of building and sought a new marriage of buildings with the landscape, but to very different effect and with very different purpose. He explains in *A Testament* (1957) that, as he looked at the human figure on the rolling Western plains,

every inch of height there on the prairie was exaggerated. All breadths fell short. So in breadth, length, height and weight, these buildings belonged to the prairie just as the human being himself belonged to it with his gift of speed. . . . As a result, the new buildings were rational: low, swift and clean, and were studiously adapted to machine methods. The quiet, intuitional, horizontal line . . . and these new streamlined, flat-plane effects first appeared together in our American architecture. . . .

With this new kind of American architecture, the house was cantilevered, long, low, tenuous, and continuous with its roof-sheltered space extending into the landscape around. Perhaps Wright is most happily remembered in the house called "Fallingwater" in Pennsylvania, a house in a forest, its cantilevered balconies and terraces reaching out over the rock slabs of the waterfall below.

Wright became the chief missionary of urban decentralization and, exalted by his own language, a somewhat confused prophet of what he called "the new life of agrarian urbanism and urbanized agrarianism." In *The Living City*, one of his many published manifestos, he argued his case thus:

In the city of today, as of yesterday, ground space is reckoned by the square foot. In the organic city of tomorrow ground space will be reckoned by the acre. No less than an acre to each individual man, woman and child. This individual acre seems minimum when we consider that if all the inhabitants of the world were to stand upright together, they would scarcely occupy the island of Bermuda. Reflect that in the United States there are about 57 green acres each for every man, woman and child within our borders at this time.

A man would be a fool, he declares, to live in a rented city, surrounded by politicians who are "promise-merchants" and lawyers who are parasites.

Wright was born in the seventies and many of his buildings have become dated because of their *art nouveau* affectations and the imprint of his cantankerous personality. Throughout a long life he poured out a torrent of histrionic evangelical persuasion, much of it in the language of the soap-box orator and much of it on the margin of nonsense. Nevertheless Wright's is unquestionably the true poetic voice that pours out the longings of the roving North American for the independent

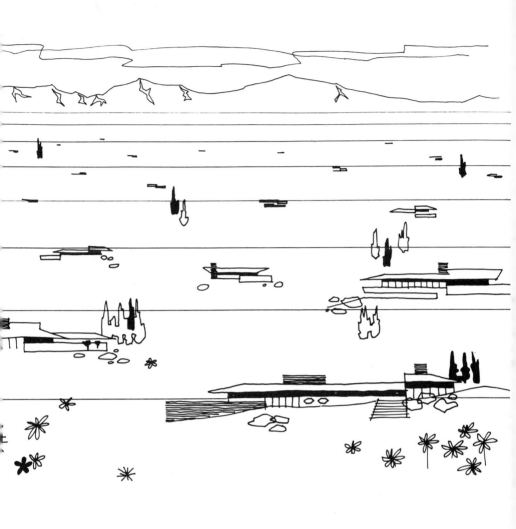

THE BROAD HORIZON OF FRANK LLOYD WRIGHT'S OPEN CITY
in the spacious American landscape

ownership of a piece of earth and the long, sheltering roof. For this reason he is a contrast with the urbane European, Le Corbusier. The American rebels against the city. The European embraces the city with respect and affection and gives it a new interpretation. The American (Wright pretentiously calls him a "Usonian") exerts his egotism through the proprietorship of home and land and by family isolationism. The European accepts the anonymity of the big city, assured of the individuality of his intellect, less dependent upon material possession.

The contrast is, of course, exaggerated; there are plenty of both kinds of people on each side of the Atlantic. The tenants of the Marseilles Block do not all have Le Corbusier's sophisticated attitude to life. Not all the ranch-house suburbanites are mavericks like F.L.W. Nevertheless the stereotypes do serve a useful purpose in distinguishing the images in people's minds as they idealize the city and its architecture. The great slabs of apartments in Regent Park and City Park, Toronto, are derived from the Marseilles Block, however inadequate may be the landscape at their feet. In the suburbs of Winnipeg and Toronto the spreading eaves and glass walls are an echo of Wright's idealization of the prairies.

What kind of city can be made out of Wright's idealization? We have his own statement of this in the imaginary plan of Broadacre City, first set out in 1934 and published again in 1958. Here are vineyards and orchards, little homes on small holdings, forming a broad tapestry over which are distributed, here and there, all the elements of urban work and life: factories and educational plant and professional offices and country clubs and merchandising centres and a shrine dedicated to "Universal worship," with columbarium, cemetery, and nine sectarian temples surrounding a central edifice. The open, rectilinear geometry and the pattern of meadows, orchards, and gardens would be intelligible from an aeroplane; but, on the ground, the effect would uncomfortably resemble the outer reaches of the suburbs where, from anywhere to almost anywhere else is a journey of several miles. This is urban sprawl *par excellence*, deliberately designed and contrived. It is as though the population of Hamilton stretched itself out through the fruitbelt of the Niagara Peninsula. It is a plan, of course, based on the streamlined mobility of the "Usonian" in his car.

Le Corbusier, on the other hand, returns to the ancient, continuing, and intimate facts of the city: to man, woman, and child on their feet. Architecture is in the spaces you walk through, the walls you touch with your hands, what you see with your eyes sixty-three inches from the ground. At the entrance to the Marseilles Block, impressed into the rough concrete, is the "modulor," the figure of man to whose measure-

1

REGIONAL CENTRE

The towering headquarters of a great urban region in a process of transformation. Montreal has a metropolitan population of more than two million, growing at the rate of more than half a million each decade. Its concentrated centre grows upwards, as the new sprawling city spreads out and consumes the surrounding farmland in the basin of the St. Lawrence River.

2

CITY STREET, OLD STYLE

The electric street-car picked up its passengers out of the snow and the mud and enabled the city to stretch out into the first suburbs, the long straight strips of street-car routes.

(2) Sparks Street, Ottawa, in 1890, a town stuck in the mud before the car tracks were laid.

(3) Toronto in 1905. The sociable street-car carried its passengers from the new suburbs to the city centre and back again, without damage to shoes and skirts.

(4) Portage and Main, Winnipeg, in 1920. Besides causing the first suburbs, the mass-transportation street-car also made the solid heart of the Canadian city, later to be submerged and scattered by the private car.

3

4

5

REGIONAL ARTERY, NEW STYLE

To link the new outlying suburbs with the regional city
centre, new routes have to be found, free of local traffic
and the interruptions of commercialized frontage. The
long, flowing lines of the Don Valley Parkway, Toronto,
follow the natural contours of the land.

6

SUBURBAN UNIFORMITY

In an industrial city where many people are employed in the same kinds of occupations, with similar incomes and with possessions purchased from standardized production-lines, there must inevitably be a good deal of uniformity of housing. But suburbs, such as this part of Toronto, have failed to provide the varieties of accommodation that are required at successive stages of life; nor has there been provision for many kinds of buildings and open spaces that are required to fulfil the social life of a community.

NEW SUBURBAN DESIGN
Model of a suburban community designed by Project Planning Associates for Central Mortgage and Housing Corporation and the Ontario Provincial government. Neighbourhoods of single-family houses, row-housing for low-income tenants, and high-rise apartments for single people and old people are clustered around a small Town Centre. Here there is variety in the choice of accommodation and the social identity of the community is focused upon its central services and parks.

URBAN SPRAWL AND SHADOW

The orchards and vineyards of the Niagara Peninsula have been invaded by disorganized suburban growth as the shadow of the city falls upon the most fertile land in Ontario. Should city people destroy their own garden? Are they willing to pay the price of its conservation?

CITY AND COUNTRY MEET

The suburban city should meet the country with a "clean" edge, without the shadow of blight upon the landscape beyond. Regional highways reach out to bridge the surrounding parkland of farms and woodlands, snowscape and summer pasture. Here city people share with farmers an interest in cultivating the land for crops and fruits and dairy products, as much for their scenic as for their food value.

THE INFINITE LANDSCAPE

Almost every Canadian city is within reach of forests and hills and water that have become an inherent element of city life. Now the winter landscape is becoming as accessible as the summer cottage and the lake. (11) The Gatineau hills near Ottawa.

City people, confined and limited by streets and buildings, have always sought the open horizon of land and sky. Ancient and modern landscape painters have expressed this yearning of city people to reach into the further world of imagination and infinity. (12) Claude Lorrain's seventeenth-century romantic "Pastoral Landscape" in the Collection of the Art Gallery of Toronto.

11

12

ments we all conform in arm and hand and head. Cities exist where people congregate to work, to do business, to eat and drink, and meet and kiss and play. Cities exist to bring people close together to engage in these personal confrontations. In the green landscape it must be a vertical city. The core of the city is in the very midst of where people live, expressed by the buildings gathered around an esplanade, a place to walk. Concentration of living implies that there is a focus of activity. In the Marseilles Block, eighteen floors high, the mid-height level is an interior "street" with stores, hotel, post office, and laundry. Every urban centre, whatever the size, contains a focal core. For Le Corbusier the highest order of focus is in the intense and talented life of Paris; less dramatic but no less important in the national life of France are the innumerable modest villages each focused upon a gathering place where rural life is assembled around co-operative and communal interests.

The contrast between the two images is not in the difference between two kinds of building, the massive vertical sculpture of Le Corbusier and the low family roofs of Frank Lloyd Wright. It is in the difference between intensity and dispersal, between the focus and the dissolution of the city.

‖‖

THE URBAN REGION

1. City and Region

THESE ARE the recollections, the images, and the idealizations of cities that come to us out of the past. From the ancient past, from the cities of Church and State, we receive firm and impressive images of people gathered around the sources of religious inspiration and secular power; in all the confusions of today's world we may indeed envy earlier city people who could see so clearly the dominating features of their lives, the temples, the cathedrals, and the palaces. From the nearer past we inherit the strong protest against the ugly brutality of industrialization, the demand for a new reconciliation of work and life; nineteenth-century romantic revivalists hoped that the virtues of authentic craftsmanship and the morality of the countryside could somehow be recaptured for city folk in their artificial environment. This sentiment reaches us in the wistful images of greenbelt and garden city, in the agrarian urbanism of Frank Lloyd Wright, and, in Canada, it reappeared again in the small-holdings programme of the Veterans' Land Act, a measure to defend the city man against the indignities of the fitful industrial economy. Out of the more recent past come Clarence Stein and Le Corbusier, still deeply involved in trying to blend the town and the green landscape, but attempting this reconciliation in the age of motors and a more sophisticated urban population.

Has the present period, more than a decade since World War II, given us no new idealizations of the North American City? No! No fresh solution of the suburban problem has appeared out of this generation. The same heroic figures still stalk the suburban landscape: Howard, Unwin, Frank Lloyd Wright, Stein, and Le Corbusier. We are still fighting their battles, though all of them formed their views in a period very different from our own. Meanwhile the present reality of the great urban region has turned out to be rather different from what anyone could have foreseen.

However, this searching of the past does help to clarify what we are looking for and does provide some models against which we can test our own objectives. Particularly it helps us to deal with three sets of questions.

First, there is the question suggested by looking at ancient cities: What are the central purposes in life that could serve as dominant themes in the arrangement of cities? It is true, of course, that the modern city is an economic apparatus that must be judged for its efficiency in supporting industrial production and employment; and for this purpose it must have access to raw materials and power and it must possess highly developed systems of traffic and communication. But the production engineering of a city is not an end in itself, only the means to an end. Presumably the end purpose is a way of life represented not by the traffic artery, the factory, and the office but by the social institutions that give meaning to life itself. The ultimate purpose of a city is to be discovered in a quality of heart and mind. How this is to be represented is a question to which we shall return later.

The second set of questions keeps on reappearing throughout the long history of cities: What is to be the relationship of the city with its surroundings? What is the nature of the boundary between city and country? How is the city to grow outwards into its surrounding hinterland? From the Utopia of Thomas More to the Garden City of Ebenezer Howard and on into the present concern for the ravaged fruitlands of the Niagara Peninsula and the destruction of the choicest farms around every big city this question has been a constant preoccupation. As city people have become more mobile, the sharp definition of the old city walls has disappeared, the edge of the suburbs is blurred and indefinable, the impact of city people spreads far and wide over a vast surrounding region. In considering the form and behaviour of cities we must now look at comprehensive urban regions, not at city and country separately.

Then, thirdly, there are the questions about the organic structure of the suburbanized city. If future suburbs, rather than being a lamented muddle, are to have some intelligible plan to guide the host of individual public and private developers, there must be some system of constituent parts. The "neighbourhood" as propounded by Clarence Perry has been generally accepted in North America as the basic component piece of suburban design. Does this fit our present circumstances? Is this idea of a systematic "planned" city in fact necessary or is it a denial of the very freedom we seek?

These questions overlap and affect one another and cannot be treated separately. But in a collective answer we may perhaps solve the riddle of the suburbs and discover the kind of future city we want to build. Let us begin by taking the broadest view of the city and its surrounding region.

City people don't stay neatly inside municipal boundaries but are immensely attracted by surrounding open spaces, where they are inclined to spread out indiscriminately and, to their own subsequent remorse, to litter the very countryside they wanted to enjoy. The shadow of the city on the surrounding landscape keeps on lengthening as you look at it. As communications stretch out, the city's presence is felt farther and farther from the centre. The countryside cannot be seen as a still picture of farms and trees and motionless figures in the landscape; it is an intense magnetic field with a powerful focus on the metropolitan centre. The magnetic force is centred upon Dorchester Street in Montreal, on University Avenue in Toronto, or on Georgia Street in Vancouver, and its strength declines as it reaches out to farms and fields and forests fifty miles away. Within this whole region four roughly concentric zones can be distinguished; in each of them the influence and the interest of the city is different. The inner zone is the built-up area of city and suburbs.

THE URBAN-CENTRED REGION

M for Metropolis, the Mass City, the Mother City

S for Suburbs, the Sprawl, the State of Shock
and the Urban Shadow

C for Country, Cultivation, Conservation and the
Co-operation of Country People and City People

R for the Region of Recreation and Natural Resources

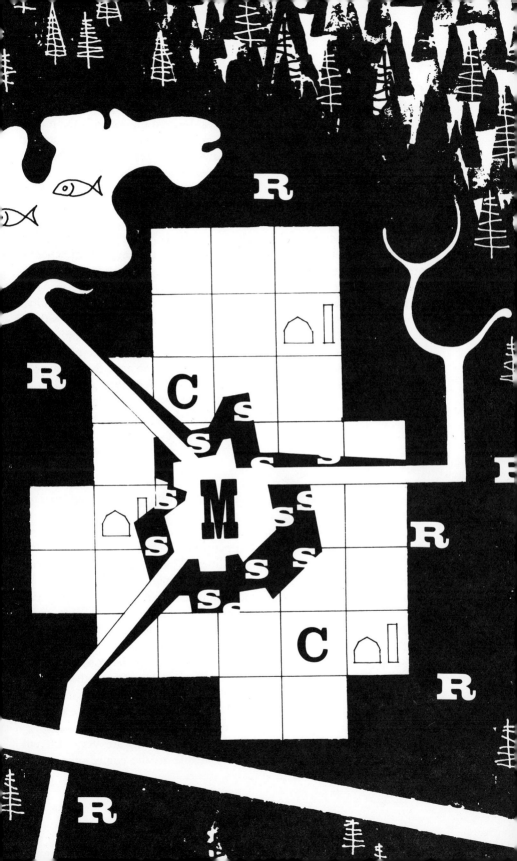

Outside the suburbs is the ring of land into which the city is growing, and beyond this is the expanse of agricultural land that nourishes the city with milk and fruits and vegetables. Beyond this again is the hinterland, which, for so many Canadian cities, is a territory of forests and water and rocks providing not only the natural resources on which the economy of the city is based—lumber and metallic ores and hydro power—but also a place for recreation in summer and in winter. This whole region of inner and outer zones must be regarded as the total setting of urban life.

The inner zone of built-up city and suburbs is Metropolis, the Mass City, the Mother City. Metropolis is composed of a number of separate municipalities and, across the continent from Halifax to Vancouver, there are political upheavals going on as each of the Canadian Mass Cities endeavours to consolidate itself into some kind of unified political society competent to act as Mother City, to watch over the growth of its new suburban communities. Some degree of internal unification would be useful anyway to manage the complex affairs of a great metropolis, its traffic and schools and housing problems. But these political upheavals in Montreal, Toronto, and Winnipeg can also be regarded as an essential prelude to a more effective system for giving birth to new communities, for directing their early growth and bringing them to maturity. So far only Winnipeg has succeeded in creating a Metropolitan City that embraces the entire suburban growth within its jurisdiction.

All the people of Metropolis have a common interest in the outer zones of their region and require to speak with a single voice in protecting their surrounding landscape from damage and to be able to reach out and possess open spaces for recreation. Scattering out over the whole region in their cars the people of Metropolis have to develop extraterritorial rights and responsibilities. What's the use of a car if you can't get to the water, the woods, and the mountains? What's the use of getting there if water, woods, and mountains are not yours to enter? For Montrealers the Laurentians are as much a part of the city's life as St. Catherine and Sherbrooke streets. Half the population of Ottawa goes up the Gatineau, to a lake in summer and for skiing in winter. The Muskoka district is as much a part of Toronto as the corner of King and Bay. Life in Winnipeg would be insupportable without the Lake of the Woods and Winnipeg Beach. What would Halifax be without St. Margaret's Bay and Vancouver without Grouse Mountain? These outermost parts of the region are pieces of the contemporary urban scene.

In this respect our expectations for life in cities are very different from the opportunities that were available to the contemporaries of

Ebenezer Howard. The whole satellite-in-a-greenbelt idea is no longer relevant to our North American circumstances because we have found other solutions to the problem of accessible open space. The satellite-in-a-greenbelt idea arose in a period when town people had to reach the country by walking there from home; consequently there would have to be a limit to the size of the town and there would be an advantage in building the town compactly in order to reduce the distance to the open country. But the terms of the problem have changed. The motor-car now offers access to an infinity of open country outside the city and has made it possible to spread out the suburbs so that house-in-a-garden has been substituted for city-in-a-garden. Instead of having to build constellations of separated satellite towns we have solved the problem with the car.

So the growth of metropolitan cities will continue to take the form of continuous expansion around the outside edges, with a belt of land always in the process of conversion from rural to urban use. This transitional zone is the scene of urban sprawl, and has also been well named the area of "urban shadow." Within the shadow of the city's looming mass, land is taken from agricultural use as farmers find themselves taxed to pay for the schools and services of newly arrived suburban families and as they decide that it is more profitable to sell out to speculators. The blight of the city's shadow is seen in the fields of unmown grass, untended fruit trees, and blowing weeds, and in the crop of commercial signs sprouting on the roadside. Canadian studies of this shadow zone have shown that the total acreage of affected land is commonly more than twice the area of the entire built-up city and, in the most wasteful situations, as much as five times the area. Unfortunately this is usually land of prime agricultural quality because thriving cities have so often begun as the market centres of rich agricultural settlements. It is unfortunate that the site requirements for raising a crop of human beings are similar to the requirements for other crops: there has to be workable ground for putting down foundations, for laying underground pipes, and for stabilizing the surface with lawns, and the land must be reasonably flat, well drained, and have an accessible water-supply. The "best" land for agriculture is also usually the "best" land for building a city.

The task of converting raw land into the form of a city has commonly been imposed upon a bordering municipality that is in a state of shock, its population half rural and half suburban, neither part having financial resources or any real motives for such a formidable undertaking. Why, say the farmers, should we pay to provide schools and services for an incoming urban population with expensive city tastes? And why, say the newly arrived, newly married suburbanites, should we pay for the next migration of similar suburbanites? The situation invites a disintegration of farming operations and discourages creative interest in the important decisions that have to be made for building a city. As a general principle, the Mother City, which attracts population, creates employment, and spawns the new suburbs, should be responsible for city-building. This zone of urban shadow should be within the jurisdiction of the metropolitan community and, as new daughter communities are settled and become established, new junior municipalities should be formed to take over local affairs.

In preparing this transitional zone to receive the growth of the city, everything should be done to reduce the withering effect of urban shadow; the tax system should not penalize farm operations for city-building purposes and land should not be cut up and converted into speculative real estate until it is finally necessary to remove it from productive rural use. The Mother City should itself acquire in advance the strategic centres of new suburban communities, the focal points of future streets and communications, the sites of new suburban Town Centres that will determine the shape and character of surrounding residential areas. The Mother City (or an agent of the Mother City) should govern this land "in trust" for the future generations that are going to live there but are not present at the time of city-building. This is an arrangement analogous with the Canadian federal government's responsibility for northern territories while they are being raised to the status of self-governing provinces.

Immediately outside this ring of urban shadow is the cultivated landscape of farms and fields, woodlots and rivers, which forms the domestic environment of our great cities. This is the garden of the city, the country estate, the home park, the whole rural scene that sweetens the lives of city people besides providing nourishment in milk and vegetables. The historic water-front settlements along the St. Lawrence and Riche-lieu rivers, the old Ontario concession roads back from the shores of the Great Lakes, the richest black earth of Manitoba, and the dwindling farmlands in the Fraser Valley—all of these now have a new and added value as part of the life of Montreal, of the great Ontario cities, of Winnipeg, and of Vancouver. City people and the farming population now share an interest in conserving and improving the property that our forefathers cultivated for many generations. The presence of the metropolis imposes new city-serving features on this zone: parkways and freeways for city access and egress, as well as places where city people can enjoy rivers and hills and woodlands. City people have to share the use of the land and must do so without hindering the farmer's work, damaging his fences, or destroying the scenery with their untidy habits and the greedy blight of city advertising. To protect and conserve this common estate the metropolitan community must join with the rural municipalities in planning highways and parks for city people. This requires a form of regional authority such as has been set up for the Edmonton District and for other urban-centred regions in Alberta, where the provincial government and local people share the costs equally.

The most difficult question to be decided in the management of this zone of the urban region is the amount of new population that should be admitted, to increase the size of small rural centres and to scatter new settlements on the landscape. Should ex-urbanites and dormitory communities be welcomed and provided for? What, in fact, is to be the attitude towards the spontaneous growth of new satellite cities-in-the-garden, whether following the model of Ebenezer Howard or by the enlargement of existing small towns? There has been a long tradition of encouragement for the decentralization of cities, favoured by romantic and escapist sentiments, by a sturdy distaste for big cities, and by the status symbols of station-wagons and saddle-horses. But with the present unstable and volatile nature of the metropolitan city perhaps we should reverse this attitude in the effort to confine and isolate the territory of urban shadow and to restrain the inevitable withering of the rural landscape.

It has been stated that, at the present rate at which Canada's metropolitan cities are consuming the land around them, the very best agricultural land in Canada will soon be covered with streets and houses and shops and industries. By the year 2000 A.D., asserted Mr. A. D. Crerar at the Resources for Tomorrow Conference (in October, 1961), there will be virtually no agriculture left in the lower Fraser Valley, or in southern Ontario between Cobourg and London, or in the lower St. Lawrence Valley between Cornwall and Three Rivers; this would inevitably occur, he calculated, if there were no interruption in our economic expansion and population growth and if our present sprawling habits of urban life should continue.

Among agriculturalists and economists there is not yet a consensus of opinion about the ultimate significance of this fearful loss of Canada's natural resources. Should it be regarded as a calamity that threatens our national survival or does it simply present a technological challenge to raise the productivity of inferior soils? Is this just the price we have to pay for the advantages of living in big cities with all their culture and the convenience of their mass-produced products? Whether it is a matter of economic survival or simply a question of conserving, for our future use and enjoyment, the garden that surrounds each city we can at least choose policies for city growth that will not wilfully destroy a most precious possession. Most Canadians live close to the edge of the rocky Canadian shield or under the lea of the Western mountains or not far from the arctic wastes and they can ill afford to lose the best cultivated land along the southern border. Consequently we should try to limit the sprawl of the suburbs and keep the surrounding land as free as possible of ex-urbanites, dormitory subdivisions, satellite towns, urban squatters, and all the city influences and commercial pests that erode and blight our own garden.

It is, of course, this closeness of the hinterland of rocks and forest and mountains and wilderness that gives a unique and incomparable quality to Canadian city life, a dimension that far exceeds what is possible in any model garden city and greenbelt, and makes Ebenezer Howard's vision seem modest indeed. We should begin to think of our great metropolitan centres not just as city places but as all-inclusive regions containing both the city and its outlying possessions in the woods and on the lakes, a kind of commonwealth. But in order to fulfil this larger conception of a city, the problems of metropolitan unity must first be solved so that the total interests of city people will be represented in the extraterritorial parts of this commonwealth.

Fortunately we have a most effective demonstration of how this might be accomplished, for there is one Canadian metropolis that already possesses an agency to give all its citizens access to the nearby hills and forests, by means of a system of parkways that starts at the border of the city and penetrates into an incomparable recreation country. The National Capital Commission is, in effect, a metropolitan body that serves the whole community of Ottawa and Hull, and for the benefit of the city population it has developed its splendid driveways into the Gatineau Hills. The circumstances are, of course, unique because the Commission is supported by federal government funds; but it serves to illustrate how other metropolitan regions could establish agencies to reach out into the spacious playgrounds that should be accessible to all Canadian city-dwellers.

2. Constituent Parts of the City

HAVING TAKEN A BROAD VIEW of the city and its surrounding region let us consider the internal organization of the suburbanized city, to discover how it could best be arranged into a system of constituent parts. What, in fact, do city planners usually do in preparing for the growth of the city into the surrounding zone of urban shadow?

After surveying and mapping the configurations of the land and making an inventory of its resources and sites, the city planner usually starts by setting out the broad distinctions between land to be used for industry, land for residential use, and what can be left as open space for recreation. Having mapped out the land with this broad brush the suburban planner then sets out a pattern of neighbourhood areas, indicating the approximate positions of future primary schools and the general framework of main streets. Against this background a Planning Board is able to examine proposals for land subdivision and justify their approval or rejection. Bit by bit the pieces of the jigsaw puzzle are fitted together to make a whole picture; each scrap of street system must fit on to the next and what is built on one patch of land must not conflict with what is going to be built on the adjoining patch.

"Neighbourhood Planning" is generally recognized in Canada and the United States as the arrangement of local streets, open spaces, and family housing in relation to a school for young children. It provides a convenient basis for the division of the vast residential expanse of the suburbs into a reasonably small-scaled cellular structure. The educational system imposes a roughly uniform distribution of elementary schools and so disciplines land subdividers, housing developers, and town planners. The street plan can be contrived to protect children from traffic hazards on their daily journeys to and fro; at best there may even be a system of foot-paths through park strips, as in Don Mills and Kitimat. Though neighbourhood plans are often poorly designed and executed, yet no one would dispute the principle involved here, any more than they would question the advisability of installing a bathroom in every house.

However, as a basic cellular system for the suburbs, neighbourhood planning does not fulfil all the requirements of social diversity and integration. It provides a logical arrangement of family homes and elementary schools, but it does not offer any obvious place for households at other stages in the cycle of life. And, unfortunately, there has been a further exclusiveness in the rejection of any forms of family housing that do not fit the stereotype single-family home. Younger families, older families, and poorer families who require row housing and other kinds of rental accommodation have not been welcomed as good neighbours in "neighbourhoods."

As originally conceived by Clarence Perry for the New York Regional Plan, a "neighbourhood" was a small, self-contained community focused not only on an elementary school but also on a group of churches and other social institutions, forming a community centre. At the same time he banished the shops and apartment buildings to the arterial streets on the border of the neighbourhood. Consequently, there is an inherent contradiction in Perry's plan: he wanted the heart of the family neighbourhood to be a quiet, traffic-free place and at the same time he wanted it to be an active community centre. If a neighbourhood is to be free of traffic-bearing activities, clearly the focus of community life must lie outside this scale of social unit. So we have to conclude that the neighbourhood is only a minor piece in the making of the city and should be a part of some larger whole.

The population that supports one elementary school is not large enough to support the principal social and commercial services on which suburban life depends. The populations of three or four neighbourhoods together provide a reasonable economic demand for these services: the shopping centres, places of gathering and entertainment, and clusters of apartment houses. It is just these features of a city's living areas that are generally considered alien to family neighbourhoods; every day newspapers report the vigorous resistance of home-owners to the intrusion of such activities into the sacred territory of parents and children.

A comprehensive system for residential areas must, therefore, be conceived at a scale larger than the neighbourhood, so that it can embody all the essential features of suburban living which are extra-territorial to the neighbourhood. This is the scale at which Howard's Garden City was visualized, to contain four neighbourhoods around its civic centre. This is the scale at which Radburn was originally designed, to embody three neighbourhoods. This is the scale of Don Mills in Toronto, the most coherently planned Canadian suburban community, composed of four neighbourhoods. This is the scale of Kitimat and of the British satellite towns built since World War II: Stevenage, Harlow, Crawley, and others. At this scale a community is comprehensive, with a full range of age-groups in the population, and a full roster of social and commercial institutions. In fact, ever since the Garden City idea was first launched, most of the serious attempts to create model communities have been based on the "town" scale of design.

The advantages of the full "town" scale are clear enough. But unfortunately the importance of this conclusion has been obscured by the fact that most model communities have taken the form of separate and distinct new towns, rather than being part of the metropolitan suburbs. There have been a number of reasons for this:

1. It has been extremely difficult and expensive to assemble large

enough pieces of land within the suburban fringes to carry out idealistic experiments in town design. Also, experimenters have tended to avoid the climate of suburban real estate operations where it might be difficult to withstand the pressures to conform to conventional standards and compromises. For this reason the noble experiments of Garden Cities and Greenbelt Towns have usually been withdrawn from the battleground of the suburbs and have sought the more tranquil meadowlands beyond the reach of the city. Don Mills, well within the suburban fringe of Toronto, has been a notable exception and has won a well-earned reputation for thus challenging the suburban establishment on its home ground (not without some painful experiences for its promoters).

2. In many cases the opportunity to carry out a model design has been coupled with a deliberate policy to remove population out of large, congested cities. This was the declared aim of the original Garden City idea and has been a primary motive behind the building of the British New Towns outside London and other major industrial centres. The purpose has been quite specifically *not* to add suburban extensions but to make an absolute physical separation between the parent metropolitan city and its new satellite.

3. Some towns on remote sites have presented special opportunities for the design of model communities. The people in a town that is far-removed from the amenities of big cities have a particular need for a congenial environment. Their employers are anxious to provide this environment so as to hold together a stable labour force; and since the employers usually own the entire townsite they are able to fulfil their own plans. This was the situation in Kitimat, built by the Aluminum Company in a mountain basin of northern British Columbia. Elliot Lake, based on the mineral resources of the Canadian Shield in the hinterland of Lake Superior, was developed by the provincial government of Ontario in the interests of the mining companies. Perhaps the future town of Frobisher on the remote windswept terraces of Baffin Land will be an even more dramatic example of both the opportunity and the motive to build a model community. The same motives have inspired the care given to the design of Deep River, Ontario, the atomic energy town on the banks of the Ottawa River, and to the design of the Town of Oromocto in New Brunswick for military personnel. It is possible to provide compensations for being deprived of the enjoyments of the big city.

Here are three quite different circumstances in which model communities at "town" scale have been geographically separated from a parent city; in most of these cases there has also been a reason for introducing the notion of a greenbelt. In the fulfilment of the Garden City idea the greenbelt was, of course, an inherent part of the main objective: it was to provide an accessible open space surrounding the new urban settlement (the city-in-a-garden idea), in order to restore the sentimental union of Town and Country. Also, a greenbelt acts as a kind of no-man's-land around any satellite town, to prevent its growing beyond its designed size and so upsetting all the carefully calculated proportions of its internal services and spaces. Strangely enough the greenbelt idea also turns out to have a useful application to towns in remote wilderness areas where there is always a danger of squatters, odd-balls, parasites, and secessionists settling on the outskirts and building shacks and marginal enterprises that become a blight on the high endeavours of the town. Arvida and Ajax have both been threatened in this way. It has usually been necessary to acquire a site larger than the immediate needs of town-building, in order to protect the surrounding landscape.

For these reasons most of the notable experiments in town design have involved both physical separation from a parent city and the provision of a greenbelt. This has unfortunately tended to obscure the value of these experiments in their application to suburban growth. The important fact is that only at the scale of a town, rather than at the scale of a neighbourhood, is it possible to provide a systematic arrangement of living communities. The town is the essential component part of which the metropolitan city must be constructed.

3. Nucleus and Anti-Nucleus

IN THE MODERN, SPRAWLING URBAN REGION, centrifugal forces have caused the city to fly away at the edges. To compensate for this loosening of the magnetic field it is now necessary to generate new centripetal forces around subsidiary Town Centres in the suburbs. On the strength of these new focal points will depend the whole systematic arrangement of the surrounding suburbs. What elements in the suburban city can be given this magnetic effect? What are the purposes of life that draw suburban people together?

We are not concerned here with the economic purposes which, in the first place, gather people into big urban regions. These purposes are symbolized by the downtown central business district, which is the dominating focus of the whole metropolitan region. Nor would anyone consider trying to build a suburban community around a group of industrial buildings, though industrial production is the motive of the worker, both employer and employee. In the suburbs the important purposes are in the lives of people as citizens, as individuals in the stream of regenerating life, receiving knowledge from the past and passing on the arts of living in new forms to the future.

When the new town of Kitimat was being designed in the magnificent mountain scenery of British Columbia, with Clarence Stein as consultant, there was considerable discussion about placing the townsite on the mountain slopes overlooking the Aluminum Company's industrial plant and harbour so as to give a sense of action to the community; but the site finally chosen is several miles from the plant and people's private lives are to this extent removed from their economic attachment. And there is the case of Don Mills. Here the site includes industrial land where architects have designed a number of delightful buildings in beautifully maintained landscaped spaces; in fact the quality of design for industry is superior to much of the architecture in the domestic parts of Don Mills. But in spite of this interesting reversal of the amenities of industrial and residential property it is clearly quite correct to have put the industrial land on the exterior of the site. In a suburbanized city region with great mobility and a high degree of flexibility in employment, there is likely to be little relationship between the places where people work and where they live. The social structure of the city cannot be built around centres of employment. The fact that families draw their incomes from a business machine factory, a publishing house, a pharmaceutical company, or a television plant does not represent any social identification.

Workers and their families used to live on the very threshold of their labours—on the farm, "over the shop," or under the shadow of the factory chimneys. But the evolutionary processes that have created the modern suburbanized city have separated the two sectors of life: producer and consumer; worker and citizen; employee and householder. Now a person can live in the east end of town and work in the west end. His next job may be downtown or in a plant that has moved to an industrial estate on the edge of the city. Industries are attracted to large urban regions because they can draw upon the whole labour pool. Workers are drawn to big cities because there are the widest choices of jobs and many opportunities for advancement by moving from one job to another. This freedom of the labour market occurs because the place of work is no longer hitched to the place of residence.

The modern city has shaken loose and separated its working parts from its living parts. The planning of the residential city, the city of consumers, citizens, and householders, has its own validity without reference to the working part of the city, the city of factories and offices.

It may be said that we have lost something by living apart from the places where we work and justify ourselves as effective contributors to the economic support of society. The farmer can look out from his front door over the well-tilled fields, contemplate his handiwork, and win the respect of his wife and children through this evidence of his manly abilities. It is one of the complaints about the suburbs that they lack any view of the sterner realities of life; children are raised in this sterilized vacuum without an opportunity to comprehend the true nature of life that demands hard work, skill, and organization. The suburbs are too bland. But, on mature consideration, fathers should not have regrets for this removal of their working lives from the context of the residential city. For the kind of work most of us do is no longer likely to impress our children with a sense of the nobility of labour. To operate the tools of modern industry and business requires mind rather than muscle; to children, intellectual skills seem less dramatic than the prowess of farmer, fireman, and western bandit.

Our private lives in cities do not revolve around the places where we work. The focal points in the residential city must be contrived out of the interests people share as consumers, citizens, and householders. These interests take physical form in the institutions that serve a community: in shops and schools and meeting-places. So the key pieces we are seeking, to give social structure and physical shape to the suburbs, may take the form of Town Centres, each a focal point for a group of Neighbourhoods. The size of each Centre will depend on whether there are three or four or five Neighbourhoods (about 15,000 or 20,000 or 25,000 people) in each area. The communities assembled around these Centres need not be separated by any defined boundaries or greenbelts; they may merge and overlap. The Town Centres will stand out from the suburban background as expressions of society's common interests and

ABSTRACTION OF THE CONTINUOUS CITY I
in non-nuclear, inorganic form:
an expression of accident, violence, and instability

purposes in life. Thus there will be a return to the same motives that have always brought people to the gathering-places in towns, to the Squares and Piazzas and Grandes Places, where shops and restaurants and fountains provide colour and music, where churches and statues and inscriptions encourage solemn memories. Though all kinds of outward forms have changed, though our architecture, our dress, our vehicles, and our manners have a different style, yet our social instincts and enjoyments are not so greatly changed. *Plus ça change, plus c'est la même chose.*

This gathering-together of the principal social elements of the suburban town seems to offer a rational system for reconstituting suburban society and its environment, if we could devise a workable method of planning and building such Centres.

There is, however, a contrary argument that deserves consideration. Suppose, in a nihilistic mood, that the whole notion of system and logic in the arrangement of a city is itself superfluous. Suppose that this smacks of an eighteenth-century paternalism and has the air of an archaic science. Suppose, in fact, that the very absence of any system in the suburbs were to be regarded as a freedom from the restraints of social organization and part of the liberty we have won. This kind of "anti-nucleation theory" comes to light partly as an isolationist defence against too-rich doses of sentiment about community organization, togetherness, and all synthetic forms of gregarious behaviour. And partly this view stems from a realization of the great changes that have been wrought upon society by all the means of communication that have removed barriers of space. The anti-nucleation argument denies that there really are any benefits in arranging the suburbanized city round focal centres. The argument runs somewhat as follows.

A great break-through has occurred in the nature of life in cities; the apparently aimless sprawl of suburban regions is a spontaneous and quite appropriate reflection of this change. The very lack of organized arrangement, so the theory runs, is not something to be resisted but indeed represents a kind of release from established social systems and conventions of city living. In several ways the new forms of communication have reduced the significance of geographical space. It doesn't any longer matter where your friends live because their houses can be reached quickly by car even if they are at the other end of town. Also within driving range are the widest choices of shops and entertainments and churches and all kinds of city amenities. In fact the opportunity to use a car is a pleasure—one can enjoy the feel of it on the road, see the town, and compare other people's status symbols. Then there is the telephone. The most intimate friendships can be sustained and nourished at a moment's notice through the telephone. The closeness of the ear and the mouth to the telephone seems to invite a cosiness of personal relationships which may even be shattered by the actual presence of the other party. The whole vast spider's web of telephonic friendships that our wives and daughters and sons have constructed across the city is one of the marvels of city life. "The girl next door" and the gossip opportunities of the back fence have lost their meaning. Geographical propinquity is no longer a prime consideration. The city is a universe within which everyone is in the immediate presence of everyone else.

Television, too, has depreciated the value of the local community by extending relationships into a far larger society. Now everyone is instantaneously on the receiving end of national and international news, which makes local affairs seem like very small potatoes. Everyone shares the artificial friendliness of the familiar TV personalities who are projected into our homes and seem to fulfil many of the needs for personal relationships. Those winning smiles of Fred and Joyce and John are surely directed straight at me. They make me feel confident, loved, and relaxed and I have no need to go outside to find friends and neighbours. I feel myself in the embrace of the nation which surrounds me. Real-life people are not so winning and encouraging and flattering. Real life is awkward and embarrassing.

Another "anti-nucleation" influence has been the great emphasis placed upon the individual as a member of the family, rather than as a member of society. This is manifest in the vehement dedication to home-ownership and to the single-family house as a self-contained island in the great spaces of the city; there, secure against the intrusion of neighbours and outsiders, each family group turns in upon itself. (Perhaps the current interest in the internal-courtyard house is a new expression of this indifference to the outside world.) It has been observed that purchasers of houses are surprisingly indifferent to what lies outside each lot. They are prepared to accept all kinds of external inconveniences, such as a long drive to work, lack of services, and the most ugly surroundings. Their whole concern is to concentrate upon the business at hand, the raising of a family within the boundaries of the home. When the car is put away for the night and the front door closed, the family is an anonymous part of the great telecommunication system, unconscious of the proximity of neighbours and neutral to the neighbourhood environment. "The door of the cage we call a city has been left open," declared Frank Lloyd Wright (see *Frank Lloyd Wright on Architecture*, 1941).

The young . . . can now go out as they are qualified to go. In our United States of America we are beginning to find practical realizations of our ideal of freedom in the fact that spaciousness is the great modern opportunity, that human scale is now entirely different—10 to 1 extended at least—and that we no longer need to live on little plots of ground with our toes in the street and a little backyard behind us with a few plants in it, shaking hands out of the windows on either side with neighbours good or neighbours bad. . . .

I do not believe in any "back to the land" movement; I think that any backward movement would be folly; but if, turning away from excess urbanization now, we can go forward with all that science has provided for us, going forward intelligently to the new free forms which must be made for the accommodation of life so that [we] may live more generously, more spaciously and more fully, we shall be dealing—practically—with the problem now on our hands. The future we see is our present.

These are the "anti-nucleation" arguments supporting the view that ubiquitous mobility and telecommunication have now released us from any conventional forms of city organization. The city is an abstract continuum like an infinite non-objective painting without recognizable shape or focus; or it might be thought of as plasma in which individuals and families float in a kind of unattached suspense.

It is a plausible and sophisticated point of view. True, we have been released from the cage of the congested centralized city and won the freedom of elbow-room in the suburbs. But does the pursuit of space necessarily have detachment as its objective? Social detachment as a quality of freedom has never turned out to be a great satisfaction. Freedom is the liberty to make our own choices of attachment and detachment, when and where we like. Freedom includes the opportunity to find new destinations for our roaming, new pleasures, and new purposes in life. It includes the opportunity to make the city in a new image, with a quality to inspire the devotion that people have always felt for home. So far, the freedom of mobility has been a destructive influence. We have run away from what we didn't like in cities. If city life is to be worth while we must rediscover what is positive, attractive, and dynamic in drawing people together in cities.

ABSTRACTION OF THE CONTINUOUS CITY II
in nuclear, animated form:
an expression of purpose, reason, and devotion

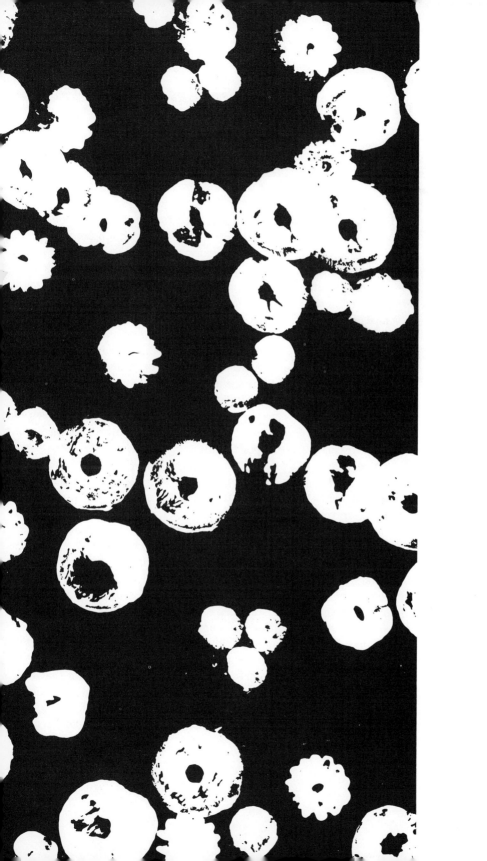

4. Communities within Metropolis

CITIES OF OUR TIME are evidently governed by two kinds of gravitational force: forces of concentration and forces of dispersal, forces of nucleation and forces of anti-nucleation. These two kinds of force are at work upon the material of the city, transforming its nature and rebuilding it in a new form.

There is a double image, two layers of city superimposed one upon the other. On one plane is the Metropolis, dispersed loosely around the central core in a kaleidoscopic abstract pattern. And, on another plane, within this sprawling region, are many residential communities each trying to cluster around its own core of local institutions. The two layers join together to give the composite picture: the loose, informal pattern of the Metropolis with points of community concentration standing out against this abstract background.

The Metropolis consists of three elements: the network of communications, the central core, and the whole scatter of businesses and services that have taken positions on the network of communications. Let us examine each of these separately.

The communications network is the whole intricate spider's web of highways, arteries, freeways, and parkways that spreads through the entire area, making every point almost equally accessible from every other point. Part of this network is the system of communications in telephone, television, and electrical power; also the metropolitan newspapers and the complex fabric of associations and organizations that knit together the human activities of the urban region. The network spreads continuously as the region grows, extending over the whole field in which the forces of dispersal and concentration operate.

The regional centre, the downtown of the big city, is the headquarters of financial and business affairs, the executive centre for public and private enterprises throughout the Metropolis and a wide region beyond. The old downtown district has been elevated and concentrated in its new role; the cluster of new office buildings proclaims that at the managerial nerve-centre of the urban economy there is no substitute for direct, personal, face-to-face communication. Besides the office buildings there are the downtown shops, hotels, and places of entertainment that seek the same customers and draw upon the same elite talents in management and performance. The central skyscrapers of Montreal, Toronto, and every other major city on the continent clearly show that the forces of dispersal do not erode this central concentration; it becomes more dramatic each year. The impressive growth of the Dorchester Street complex of buildings in Montreal and the array of businesses on University Avenue, Toronto, is a new phenomenon. They are not part of the original financial centres on St. James Street and Bay Street, nor are they part of the earlier downtown shopping districts. They represent a new feature of the regional city, a kind of management centre.

The third element of the Metropolis is the whole scatter of industries, businesses, and services throughout the area served by the communications network. Dispersal rather than concentration is an advantage to certain urban operations that can gain space and accessibility by not being at the centre. As long as they are placed somewhere on the communications network their exact location may not be a matter of much consequence since almost every position on the network is almost equally accessible by modern transportation. There may be a tendency for some industries and businesses of kindred nature to form new clusters at outlying points on the network, but isolation also has its advantages. For example, a university or a hospital centre or a research campus may be completely detached from any other activity. Airports and regional shopping centres have to be placed on the regional network of communications but are best separated from other traffic concentrations. And, finally, there are the motels and automobile services that feed upon the network itself.

This is the kaleidoscopic Metropolitan City, continually changing and adapting itself to new technological and economic conditions. New functions appear in detached places on the communications network and, at the same time, new buildings ascend at the concentrated centre. The busy, glittering, heroic Regional City flatters us with the realization that we belong to a large, sophisticated society. The spreading traffic network offers the greatest liberty to come and go and reach out into the countryside beyond. We exult in this freedom and nobility that transcends the little scale of home.

Yes, we have been released from the cage of the congested, conventional, centralized city.

But there is another city, on another plane, a place scaled down to the size of man, woman, and child. The unfolding of individual lives requires a smaller and more substantial base than the sprawling universe of business and trucks and work and communications and management. The Metropolitan City is a stimulating external environment, but a good place in which to stay and live must have a more static and focused character. Our private lives thrive on personal relationships that are companionable rather than gregarious, arm-in-arm rather than bumper-to-bumper. The events and scenes of daily life evoke emotions of attachment and possession, memory and continuity. People and places become identified with one another. If we have become restless gypsies in the modern city it is not for the lack of the primitive desire to become attached to a place; it is because the physical form of the community in the suburbs has not commanded attention and devotion.

Within the great Regional City people look for a place to live that has concentration and meaning and permanence. Forces of dispersal may govern the physical Metropolis but the people themselves have a natural inclination to gather around centres of human attachment.

IV

TOWN CENTRES

1. Acquiring the Public Land

PROMOTERS OF SHOPPING CENTRES were the first to try and recapture for the suburbs some of the traditional delights of cities. Stores have been grouped around a pedestrian mall, paved, landscaped, and decorated with flowers and fountains to recall some of the charm of European cities. You have to get rid of the car to enjoy the Piazza San Marco, the Rue de Rivoli, the Spanish Steps, or Piccadilly. The introduction of the pedestrian Mall into new Shopping Centres and into old downtown shopping districts like Sparks Street in Ottawa has been an effort to restore a sociability that cities had lost.

The promoters of these centres have, indeed, been so aggressive in placing themselves in new suburban areas that the local shopping centre has asserted a claim to be regarded as the true social focus of the community. It has won this position by default, because these private developers, seeing the immediate needs of people in the suburbs, have been quick to respond to them. They have evolved a new type of package-deal enterprise, to acquire the strategic site, to design and construct the shopping centre, and to move in rapidly with a complete roster of retail services.

This has been a nervous, successful, and stimulating feature of suburban growth. The very pace at which it has occurred is due to the explosive force that has shattered the metropolitan community, and consequently the shopping centre has come to be divorced from the other elements of community life. Public enterprise cannot move at the volatile pace of private enterprise; it requires a longer time to gather its will, its strength, its funds, and to put its plans into action. People have to have coffee and cornflakes tomorrow morning but it may be ten years before they are ready to build a church. They need hardware and drugs and smokes this week-end but they may not feel the need for a library, an auditorium, and a public garden for quite a few years. Yet it is all these things put together that make a permanent Town Centre which will not just attract business but will also enable all such public and private enterprises to give each other mutual support.

As population begins to gather in each new suburban area the site for its focal centre should be prepared, with adequate space to receive the pieces it will contain. The daily marketing services will naturally come first, as soon as the hungry families are assembled. The public services will follow in response to the demand of the population for arrangements for education, recreation, and other social amenities. And, finally, there will gradually appear the institutions created by the people within the community as they get to know one another and a new unit of society seeks to express its identity. There is thus a timing problem in holding together a site on which these features can be given an appropriate place; to ensure such a site is a tactical responsibility of those engaged in the administration and design of rapidly growing cities; it requires a new kind of collaboration between public and private enterprise.

There is a still further horizon of time that we ought to consider in the building of Town Centres: the longer time-span of history. Amidst all that is impermanent and ephemeral about our cities, can there not be a place where we can leave a permanent record of our own time? North Americans live in cities that are going through a shattering process of transition and in an age that encourages change and replacement and novelty. Few of our cities have had a very long history and we have not inherited a great deal of remarkable beauty in architecture and civic design, so we are inclined to be sceptical of monuments and our taste in architecture is light-hearted and prefabricated. Yet we cannot help regretting this ephemeral attitude when we look at cities of other times and other places, which fascinate us just because of the record of history that is built into them. We envy those who raised the columns and towers and monuments in ancient cities, for their unquestioning assumption that these would be there forever. What of our own place in the span of history? Much that we build today is improvised for the moment, planned for obsolescence, and will surely be removed and replaced by our grandchildren. Can we leave nothing permanent behind?

Here, in the environment of the suburbanized city, we might rediscover the sense of history that pervades the town squares and piazzas of other times. Surrounded by the ever changing, evanescent urban region, a Town Centre could be a place for permanence. Its trees are here to stay. The stone slabs in the paving will be worn by the feet of many generations. Occasions will be remembered in sculpture and inscription. This is the place where ancestors and descendants can establish their central beliefs and endeavour to pass them on through the beauty and stability of what they have built.

To fulfil this conception of a Town Centre, to assemble open spaces and plan public architecture which will express the life and traditions of a growing community—this requires a long-term public interest in the property. The acquisition of the site and the management of the Centre must be the responsibility of a public trustee, for a number of reasons.

First of all, there is the problem of timing. It is difficult to bring together in one place the constituent pieces of a Town Centre, the private businesses and public institutions, because they reach maturity at different times. There may be a gap of several years between the appearance of retail businesses and of churches and other social institutions. Ultimate success in bringing the Centre to its complete form will thus depend on public responsibility for holding sites "on ice" for the more slow-moving enterprises; it must be recognized that their development needs encouragement and their entry into the Town Centre campus must be secured at a reasonable land cost.

Secondly, there is the character of the Town Centre, as an expression of the paramount interest of the public and as the social capital of the community. The surrounding territory of this new suburban city will be divided among a multitude of individual owners, and each property will be dedicated to the private enjoyment and advantage of its owner. The Town Centre land should have a different quality. Here even commercial property must be planned for public use. The design of landscape and buildings and the policing of the property are matters of public responsibility and determination. The architectural composition of the buildings in the Centre should be regarded as an exercise in civic design; there need be no suppression of liveliness in architectural style but the design should recognize the community's continuity in time. This is the setting for fine architecture of permanent value rather than for passing fashions. This characteristic of civic design in the Town Centres might possibly be achieved by imposing legal controls on privately owned land and property; but it is likely to be more successful where the land itself is publicly owned and released for private use only upon fulfilment of certain designs.

Thirdly, there is a problem of monopoly. If the site of a suburban Town Centre is designated in advance of the frontier of suburban growth the land will immediately start to acquire an inflated value. The owner of that particular property is, in effect, granted a monopoly and is in a position to set a special price on such a strategic location. Attempts to plan new suburban areas have been continually frustrated by this problem: the very act of designating a strategic location on a city plan, the identification of the "best" sites, automatically places a high value on this land. Consequently purchasers cannot afford these sites for the very purposes they should fulfil. This has been one of the contributory causes of the dispersal of the suburbs, the scattering and leap-frogging to cheaper land. The economic conditions are unfavourable to concentration. It is therefore axiomatic that if the sites of Town Centres are to be predetermined by the will of the community, through plans made by local governments, the sites must be placed in public ownership. To compel public and private organizations serving the community to purchase expensive land within the limited space of Town Centres would be inequitable and unworkable. If it is in the public interest to bring about a concentration of community services the economic disadvantages of concentration must be removed. This can only be done effectively by public acquisition of the sites and the disposal of sites at fair and reasonable prices.

And finally, the fourth reason for public ownership of these sites is a corollary of the previous argument. The value that is placed upon land at the strategic centre of any community is created by the community itself; it is a consequence of all the public and private investment that has gone into building the housing and streets and underground services of a residential area. The presence of the surrounding population creates the market for the land and the services performed at the centre. Hence there is a legitimate opportunity for the community to recapture some of the value that it has itself created. This was the underlying economic thesis of the original Garden City proponents who advocated the public acquisition of the entire site of each new town. In the present North American political climate this principle could not be applied to the whole private-enterprise, home-ownership sector of our suburbs, but there are obvious advantages in applying the system to the "public sector," the Town Centre. A large proportion of the land within Town Centres would, of course, simply be a regrouping of sites which would, in any case, have had to be acquired for schools and parks and other public purposes. To some extent, then, no new policy is involved; what is new would be the integration of municipal land purchases instead of separate and frequently unrelated acquisitions by School Boards and Parks Boards and other separate agencies of local government. It would be a new adventure in the experience of Canadian and American local governments to embody, in their public land acquisitions, sites large enough to receive all those functions which should be consolidated in a Town Centre.

The extent to which a community can recapture some of the value it has itself created must depend upon the climate of political philosophy. Is the public willing to endorse government action in purchasing land beyond its normal requirements for schools and parks and other recognized public purposes? Would it be acceptable to include within the public acquisition some of the most valuable commercial and residential land immediately surrounding a Town Centre site? Though the whole body of taxpayers would benefit from a capital gain accruing to the municipal corporation, yet there are contradictory attitudes to the public ownership of real estate. The home-owner would presumably support such an opportunity to reduce his taxes. But commercial real-estate interests are bound to take a different attitude, jealous of their chances to win all the capital gains arising from city growth.

The powers of Canadian municipalities to assemble land for community purposes have been recognized in provincial statutes. For instance, The Planning Act, 1955, of Ontario gives authority to municipalities (Section 19) to acquire land, to sell, lease, or otherwise dispose of it "for the purpose of developing any feature of the official plan." This Act also (Section 26) provides a method by which a municipality can come into possession of community land as an inherent part of the whole process of building its suburbs. Each private developer may be required to dedicate to the municipality 5 per cent of the land being subdivided; or where there is an official plan, he may make a cash payment of equivalent value. The funds received under this arrangement "shall be paid into a special account and the moneys in such special account shall be expended only for the purchase, with the approval of the Minister, of land to be held and used by the municipality for public purposes" in accordance with the plan. The funds are to be invested and treated as a Trustee account. There has been dispute in Ontario on whether the "public purposes" could include sites for schools, libraries, firehalls, and so on, as well as for parks. And in some suburban townships there have, unhappily, been transgressions in the use of these funds. But these doubts and abuses should not becloud the real significance of the legislation in establishing a relationship between the development of private land and the requirement for a proportionate amount of community space. Public and private development should proceed in parallel.

Another source of financial aid for the public acquisition of community land is provided in federal legislation. Under Section 36 of the National Housing Act the federal government may join with a province and a municipality in purchasing land and may contribute three-quarters of the costs; the land may remain in public ownership if it is used for rental housing or any community purpose or it may be sold off at any stage of development. This measure was introduced primarily to assist in providing sites for housing families of modest income and generally to aid the coherent development of suburbs. Part of the land may be used for community purposes. The largest blocks of land acquired under this arrangement have been in the Toronto area (1,200, 500, and 550 acres), Hamilton (900 acres), Ottawa (600 acres), Peterborough (500 acres); there have been a number of smaller acquisitions in other Ontario cities. But, on the whole, Canadian cities have made little use of this important offer.

Here, then, are two ways in which municipalities could put together the public land required for Town Centres, by drawing upon the resources of private developers and of senior governments. There is a rough justice in the idea of levying a toll on private land developers to provide community sites; this is one way of repaying the public for the value it has created. But this would not really be a workable method for assembling the kind of Town Centre site we are discussing because, by the time this land levy can be applied, it may already be too late to develop an acceptable plan for the Centre; the community's planning must operate well in advance of the frontier of land subdivision. Private land developers, then, can only be a secondary source of community land. Other methods must be found. The federal and provincial governments might help in the advance assembly of land for Town Centres by acting as bankers through the waiting period, from acquisition to development. The sites could be transferred to the agencies of local government at the original acquisition price, plus the costs of interest and administration. In this way, at no ultimate cost to the senior governments, the benefits would finally accrue to the community itself, both in the reduced cost of land for schools and parks and other public property and in the profits from the sale or lease of land for other purposes in the Town Centre.

To create a well-conceived Town Centre in a growing suburban area would be a new kind of public enterprise requiring a new authority and organization to be built into the structure of local government. Each site must be carefully selected, acquired, and held in trust for the community that is yet to arrive. There must be a Trustee organization, a public corporation with powers to receive funds from the supporting governments, to negotiate with public institutions and private businesses seeking positions in the Town Centre, and, on completion of the assignment, to hand over the completed Centre to municipal government. This body would resemble other managerial agencies of local government, such as commissions responsible for public transportation, harbours, exhibitions, and so on. There would be some analogies, too, with the British New Towns Corporations, which serve to bring a whole new town into existence and then withdraw in favour of a duly elected municipal government. And there would be some analogies with the interim managements of new towns in Canada, such as the appointed officers of the "Improvement Districts" of Ajax and other embryonic Ontario municipalities. The principles are the same, though we are dealing here, not with a whole new town, but only with its operating centre.

In the larger metropolitan regions a number of Town Centres might be in the process of development simultaneously. Though each would have to be treated as a separate and distinct project from the financial point of view, yet there would be advantages in establishing a single responsible "Town Centre Development Corporation" in each metropolitan region. The accumulation and continuity of experience would be valuable. Such a corporation could work in continuing collaboration with school boards and parks boards and with private developers of shopping centres and housing projects. The plans for the Centres would have to be discussed with public transit and car-parking authorities to assure the most efficient handling of traffic. And, perhaps most important, there would be continuity in exploring the needs and testing the satisfactions of the surrounding populations. All these experiences could lead to successive improvements and refinements in the planning and execution of Town Centres.

Some impression of the number of such Centres that might be built within a ten-year period in Canada is given by the figures shown below. Based upon the recent rate at which suburban housing has been built and assuming that a Town Centre might be provided for every 5,000 housing units, it is seen that the Toronto and Montreal areas would each require about 25 Centres within a decade while Calgary, Edmonton, and Vancouver might each require half-a-dozen. Altogether about 100 such Centres could be provided in the principal urban regions of Canada during a ten-year period.

RATE OF COMMUNITY GROWTH IN ONE DECADE
IN CANADIAN URBAN REGIONS

Based on assumptions: (1) that a Four-Neighbourhood Community built around a suburban Town Centre contains about 5,000 housing units and a population of 15,000 to 20,000; (2) that about two-thirds of all new housing is in new suburban areas and could be arranged in this form, the remaining one-third being added to the existing built-up areas of cities.

	Total number of housing units built in 5-year period 1956–60	Corresponding number built in 10-year period reduced by one-third	Equivalent number of 5,000-unit communities
Calgary	21,354	28,472	6
Edmonton	18,512	24,682	5
Halifax	6,149	8,199	2
Hamilton	17,223	22,964	5
London	9,479	12,639	3
Montreal	101,772	135,696	27
Ottawa-Hull	23,782	31,709	6
Quebec	10,721	14,295	3
Toronto	91,246	121,661	24
Vancouver	42,473	56,631	11
Winnipeg	19,040	25,387	5
	369,876	493,167	97

2. Market-places

THE MERCURIAL ARTS OF MERCHANDISING continue to adapt and readapt themselves to the new geography of the suburban city. Shops are the most lively feature in the city scene in their restless pursuit of customers. They compete for the strategic positions in the street plan of the city. Like quicksilver they concentrate, scatter, and reconcentrate.

We are now witnessing a revolutionary shift in the pattern of retail locations, brought about by the tremendous stretching-out of the suburbs. The long row of small businesses along a main artery, characteristic of neighbourhood shopping only two decades ago, can no longer lure its customers out of the traffic stream. The big department store, the most popular, respectable, and enduring old lady of downtown, has had to

HEART OF THE CITY

The Piazza San Marco, Venice, pre-eminent amongst all city centres, supreme work of civic design. Here the architecture of church and state, of commerce, trade, and entertainment, confront one another under the Italian sky. Gondolas glide quietly on the canals and friends meet at noonday and night in the great space of the Piazza. Canaletto's eighteenth-century painting of "The Piazzetta" is in the National Gallery of Canada.

14

MEETING PLACE

(14) A century ago Notre Dame Street, Montreal, was the centre of the city's commu
life; shops and churches and schools brought people to congregate in one place, as depi
here by John Murray (Royal Ontario Museum). (15) Dufferin Terrace, Quebec, is Canada's
theatrical meeting-place where people of the town and visitors mingle in all seasons and all mo
Here, high on the rock of the city, there are distant views down the river to the Ile d'Orléans
to the Laurentian hills beyond. Here journeys begin and journeys end.

15

16

SHOPPING PLACE

Shopping Centres have become important social attractions in the suburbs. Most of them are crudely arranged trading places surrounded by open acres of parked cars. A few, such as the Rockland centre in suburban Montreal, have given new prospects of civic design in their architecture and sculpture. (Ian Martin and Victor Prus, architects; the fountains designed by Norman Slater.)

18

(17) The Public Library, North York, Tor◀ (James A. Murray, architect).

(18 and 19) The Library and Art Muse◀ London, Ontario, offers not only books but films and paintings to be borrowed. There◀ art classes for adults and children and spac◀ provided for concerts and discussion meeti◀

PLACE OF LEARNING

At the heart of a community should be the institutions that fulfil the thirst for knowledge and for performance. People of all ages share these resources of schools and libraries and theatres, which should be grouped together on the campus of a suburban Town Centre. (20) Williamson Road School, Toronto Board of Education. The main entrance is used by the public to reach the Swimming Pool and Gymnatorium, under the management of the Parks Department; an example of collaboration in use of community resources. (21) The courtyard of the Buchanan Building, University of British Columbia, showing the value of outdoor spaces in the design of an educational campus.

COMMUNITY OF CHURCHES

The church-on-the-hill was the outstanding landmark of many early settlements, its spire seen across the fields and welcomed as a navigating point for men in boats. (22) The old Loyalist church of St. Edward's, Clementsport, Nova Scotia. As settlements grew into towns each congregation placed its church on the main street, where it was easy to reach and there for all to see in making their choice: Presbyterian, Anglican, Baptist, or Catholic all displayed in œcumenical juxtaposition. (23) In Mahone Bay, Nova Scotia, three churches stand side by side upon the waterfront main street: Lutheran, Anglican, and United.

22

23

THE NEW CHURCHES

The most lively and original buildings in the suburban scene have been contributed by the new churches, displaying the individuality of each congregation and the inventive imagination of architects. (24) On the campus of the University of Manitoba the Anglican and Catholic college chapels stand side by side; so also could several denominations place their churches at the confluence of suburban life, in a Town Centre. (St. John's College; architects: Moody and Moore. St. Paul's College; architect: Peter Thornton.) (25) United Church, Don Mills, Toronto (architect, James A. Murray).

Cinitatis Weſtmonaſterienſis pars.

Parlament Houſe   the Hall   the Abby

THE STATE AND THE COMMUNITY

The suburbanite should have the opportunity to fulfil his political capacities in the management of local affairs; this has become increasingly difficult in the immense scale of metropolitan cities. The suburban Town Centre should be the symbol of local political responsibility, the smallest political unit within the structure of the whole national State. (26) A seventeenth-century drawing of Westminster by Wenzel Hollar (the National Gallery of Canada) showing the city clustered around the seat of government. (27) In a stage of transition from rural to urban status, few suburban areas of cities have been able to achieve a strong political focus. Here the people of Etobicoke in suburban Toronto gather to celebrate the inauguration of their municipal centre.

overcome its dignity and chase its customers out into the suburbs. Retail business has redeployed its forces in an entirely new pattern with three quite distinct types of shopping centre: the small Neighbourhood store, the substantial Community Shopping Centre, and the much larger Regional Shopping Centre based on a suburban branch of a downtown department store.

To everyone's regret the old "corner store" is disappearing, together with its friendly storekeeper and his wife and daughter. On the shelves behind the counter was almost everything you might want in a hurry, every day of the week and after dark: ice-cream and stationery, cigarettes and canned goods, magazines and emergency remedies. This was the store specially appreciated for the personal service. But it is hard to deny the greater efficiency, lower prices, and wider range of choice in the supermarket; friendship has not survived the hard facts of economics. Bert's Smoke Shop & Ice Cream Parlor *requiescat in pace.*

No satisfactory modern version of the corner store has yet appeared. Yet every new neighbourhood needs the kind of small shop that can be reached on foot and where the children can be sent on bicycle errands. Though the housewife fills her refrigerator by expeditions to the shopping centre, she is not infallible in her plans. Everyone would like a small store of this kind somewhere nearby, but no one is willing to have it next door, with children hanging around, cars parked on the street, and trucks delivering supplies. It doesn't fit easily into a group of single-family houses. Probably the most workable arrangement is a combination of small stores and a group of small apartment buildings or row-housing, the whole designed to conceal the service yard and parking space.

The chain-store grocery first appeared as a building about the size of an ordinary city lot, about five thousand square feet, and offered some four or five hundred different items of merchandise. But the food-producing industry has so multiplied the number of brands and the variety of packages that a fully equipped food market now has to place four or five thousand items on its shelves. The building itself now occupies ten times the space. And, further to multiply the costs of operating a modern grocery store, the housewife now arrives in a car and for every square foot of floor space within the building must be added four square feet of car-parking space, asphalted and illuminated. In other words the additional shelf-space and the additional car-space have multiplied twenty or thirty times the amount of land needed to operate a food store. To operate efficiently, supermarkets now must commonly occupy as much as 25,000 square feet of building with a corresponding car-park. Supporting an undertaking of these dimensions means that a store must seek the business of a community of 3,000 to 5,000 families, a population of about 20,000. To some extent, therefore, the habits of both customers and merchandisers have defeated the first aim of taking retail business out into the suburban neighbourhood. The modest grocery store has blossomed into the resplendent supermarket, and consequently can no longer settle right on the housewife's doorstep. A larger number of customers are required to support its mammoth proportions, more of them at a greater distance.

The food market thus becomes the anchor-piece of a shopping centre, attracting to itself a cluster of small stores, the whole occupying 100,000 to 150,000 square feet of building and 10 to 15 acres of land. A building group of this size is of truly urban scale and offers opportunities for interesting architectural design with an internal mall or garden plaza. In its character and in its market area it therefore fits the scale of the Town Centre in a suburban community.

The business of the Community Shopping Centre is based on the housewife's market basket. It offers a complete repertoire of the standard foods and supplies that keep a family and its home in operation. In the jargon of the trade these are known as "convenience goods"; they are the nationally advertised products that are stocked at any foodstore, drugstore, hardware store—the kind of articles that any housewife can confidently specify on a marketing list. Exactly the same articles are likely to be found in any shopping centre in any suburban community across the land. On the other hand, there are "shopping goods": articles of clothing or furniture or fashion which involve choice or taste or comparison and have to be "shopped for." Where evaluation and selection are involved it is necessary to go where the range of choice is widest, to the specialty shops and big department stores at the centre of the city— or to that newest kind of shopping place, the Regional Shopping Centre, which is in effect a detached piece of downtown.

The group of community "convenience" stores that might be placed in a Town Centre is simply a reorganization of the same services that used to appear on either side of a main suburban artery with its bus-line or street-cars. These stores have an established, secure, and fixed market in the surrounding neighbourhoods. Once the range of services has been established there is no reason for this kind of shopping centre to grow, unless there is an increase in the density of population housed in the same area. But a Regional Shopping Centre is very different and it should not be placed in a suburban Town Centre of the kind we have been discussing. A Regional Centre aims to attract customers from the widest possible market area; the larger it becomes the more it can diversify its "shopping" goods. As an extension of the downtown shopping district there is no limit to its growth and the geographical range from which it may draw traffic. It is essentially an overflow of "downtown," largely caused by traffic difficulties at the centre, in parking space and in access. It is clear that a regional function of this kind, and all the growing traffic that it might attract, would be damaging to a suburban Town Centre. The proper place for this kind of shopping business is either at the central core of the city or at some point on the regional traffic network where it would be universally accessible.

It appears to be inevitable that such an important focus of traffic must, in the course of time, attract other services and enterprises and become the hub of a new urban subcentre at a larger scale. In addressing a gathering of shopping centre developers an American speaker recently commented as follows, as reported in a bulletin of the Urban Land Institute, October 1961:

There has to be room for expansion, and you must expand your parking at the same time you expand your retailing or you will kill the goose that laid the golden egg. Further you must go into business that is completely divorced from shopping. I have in mind such things as medical buildings, amusements, office buildings and various other features that give you the completeness of the city you are building, because you are building cities. If you do not take the leadership in making room available for these other facilities—office buildings, medical buildings and other things—they will come around you anyway. They will surround your centre and in such a way as to choke it and do it harm rather than good. I say you must do this, but it is not a hardship at all because there is money to be made in doing it.

This is the authentic voice of business enterprise and is fair warning of what may happen in the suburbs if there is not intelligent planning for Town Centres and city subcentres. Until some radical invention has appeared, to dispel the space-consuming curse of the car, there will be advantages in isolating the Regional Shopping Centre from other enterprises. It should take its place on the regional freeway-arterial network, where access will be free and there is no other function to be served.

3. Educational Centres

THE PLANNING OF FAMILY NEIGHBOURHOODS is based on the assumption that 1,000 families will normally have about 500 children of elementary school age and about 50 children of kindergarten age. This statistical assumption is, in practice, subject to embarrassing deviations; in newly settled suburban neighbourhoods almost every family is likely to have a child of elementary school age—which might mean 1,000 and not 500 children. Some kind of temporary arrangement often has to be made until things have settled down to a more normal condition.

On the same kind of assumption a group of four Neighbourhoods with 4,000 families is likely to contain about 1,200 children of high school age; this is considered to be a reasonable scale at which to operate a secondary school with its more expensive equipment and specialized teaching staff. So a high school conveniently serves an area the size of a Town and, with its forty class-rooms, auditorium, and recreation space, is one of the most substantial buildings in the suburban scene, requiring a site of about twenty acres. A further importance is now given to the high school as it becomes an educational centre not only for teen-agers but also for an increasing segment of the adult population. It is now a common experience of school authorities that the evening enrolment in adult classes is as large as the day-time school population. The school is thus a focus of community life and an essential element of the Town Centre.

The way in which schools and school districts fit into the pattern of a city's plan depends upon the length of the educational process which is kept close to home, within the family neighbourhood, and the stage at which children are sent out into a larger world for their secondary education. Traditionally this break has occurred between Grades 8 and 9 when a child is thirteen or fourteen years old. However, it is now generally believed that a critical change occurs in the nature of a child at about eleven years of age and that the break in the educational sequence would better occur between Grades 6 and 7. At this point children seem to demand a further emancipation from the mother's direct control and their boisterous, dynamic, and rowdy behaviour is a manifestation of this break-through. At this point, too, the class teacher ceases to be a kind of substitute parent and classes begin to be built around teachers of special subjects. For these reasons the Intermediate or Junior High School has been introduced, usually embodying Grades 7, 8, and 9 (ages 12, 13, and 14). These years are the threshold of the teen-age period, before a child's personal interests have taken clear shape and before the choice of a career has offered a realistic target for acquiring any specialized skill. These are important years when personal problems are not automatically referred to the mother by the teacher; both geographically and psychologically boys and girls move farther away from home and are encouraged to meet their problems in a more adult fashion.

Consequently, there is now, in many areas, a regrouping of school grades into Elementary School (Grades 1 to 6), Junior High School (Grades 7, 8, and 9), and Senior High School (Grades 10, 11, 12, and 13). Consideration is also being given to grouping Grade 10 with Grades 7, 8, and 9 so that this intermediate sequence would terminate at the present legal age for school attendance, at the age of sixteen years. This rearrangement would overcome an unfortunate characteristic of the present system in which many students move into high school and, after completing Grade 10 in two years, leave at the legal age of sixteen. The student's brief experience of high school gives him a sense of incompleteness, and, for the school authorities, there is the problem of overloading at the intake and a progressive dropping-off at later stages. If the legal school age and the completion of Junior High School were made to coincide there could be a formal recognition of achievement at the end of this educational phase. A clear distinction would then appear between this general educational process and the divergent paths that are offered in the final phases of school education, one path leading through academic high school to Senior Matriculation and a university destination, and others leading through vocational, technical, and other preparation for a useful life.

The final stages of high school (Grades 11, 12, and 13) take place in schools that are not exclusively related to their surrounding residential areas but draw students from a larger city region. The stream of students proceeding to university requires a number of academic schools or collegiates. But only a very large city is able to maintain more than one Technical or Commercial High School or more than one school specializing in the fine arts.

This is not the place for a discussion of the comparative merits of educational systems from a pedagogical point of view. But these observations have to be made because educational systems are an integral part of the spatial arrangements of the suburbs. The context of the city is itself a part of education. As children advance through the school system they depart farther from home and enlarge their knowledge and daily experience of the outside world. So the merits of the three-tier school system, as compared with the familiar two-tier system, must be considered in a spatial context. There are questions of the distance to be travelled to school, what kind of route lies between home and school, and in what kind of setting the school is placed. Within the three-tier school system the Junior High School would be, in every sense, a community school through which would pass every child drawn from the surrounding neighbourhoods. The school would properly be placed in the Town Centre focus of these neighbourhoods, along with the other institutions that tie the community together.

In the study of a Canadian suburb entitled *Crestwood Heights* the authors comment that "the community is, literally, built around its schools. It is the massive centrality of the schools that makes the most immediate physical impact on any outside observer." They go on to explain that it is not by accident that this suburban community "has literally grown up around a school. This development has the same social logic as had the cathedral-centred communities of mediaeval Europe, or the chapel-governed towns of seventeenth-century New England. There could be no better indication than this central focus in the school that a great cultural shift has occurred towards a society most of whose dominant concerns are now secular."

Besides representing the community's dedicated efforts to prepare its children to enter the adult world, the school buildings are an important possession of the adults themselves, as increasing demands are made for the night-time use of the school auditorium and class-rooms. Many who have enjoyed a university education feel an ability and an appetite for further study, stimulated by later experiences in life; this is particularly the need of women living in the suburbs. At the same time the rapid advance of science compels many wage-earners to return to formal learning in order to keep abreast of the demands made upon them in their jobs. And, finally, the opportunities and increased (and sometimes enforced) leisure have opened up new interests and entertainments and and skills. For all these reasons the principal educational plant of the community is now going on a double shift. The school plant at the focus of a suburban town should perhaps be regarded as an Educational Centre rather than simply as a High School.

It used to be one of the unquestioned assumptions of life that a working man would continue to perform much the same daily routines throughout his life, that he would live in the same place and use the same tools of his trade. Whether he worked with spade, hammer, or sickle, whether on a farm or in a factory, sameness was likely to be his lot. But the patterns of work have changed. Now most occupations involve periodic changes in tools and methods and so place new demands upon the worker for greater technical knowledge. Furthermore modern businesses and industries no longer have a large horizontal layer of static routine occupations at the bottom and just a few directing minds at the top. Our organizations of production and supply tend to be in vertical echelons, which invite flexibility and enable advancement in the careers of employees. The emphasis placed on research and the parallel emphasis on staff-training are both closely related to this continuous process of shift and change. (It is not surprising that the national Employment Service should now expect that a recipient of unemployment benefits will enrol in a training course to requalify himself for entry into the changing industrial scene.) These circumstances all point to an increasing use of the community's educational plant for adult purposes.

In its architectural design the modern High School has responded to its new status as a civic building. There is often a separation between the part of the building that has a night-time public use and the class-room section, which can be closed off at night without full heating and care-taking. A main lobby entrance is provided for the auditorium and meeting-rooms, with accessible lavatories and cloak-rooms. This place of public assembly can thus become a part of the Town Centre and not just part of the teaching plant.

Finally there is the question of the High School's proximity to the shops and other features of the Town Centre. School authorities have generally preferred secondary school sites to be separated from commercial and business areas, largely for disciplinary reasons and because of the usually disorganized character of commercial areas in the suburbs. However, in a properly organized Town Centre, where emphasis is placed on civic character in the design of buildings and landscape, there would be an opportunity to cultivate appreciation and respect for the heart of a community. The Town Square would be a campus of some solemnity as well as a place of bright lights, restaurants, and theatre. Here would be the swimming pool, the library, and the doctors' offices. Here also there would be old people out to enjoy the sunshine and people on their way to church for christenings, weddings, and funerals. This confluence of people's lives would surely be an important part of education.

4. Glebe Land for the Churches

IN THE MAKING of the new suburbs the churches have proved to be lively and thriving institutions. Even if they were to be judged by nothing more than the scale of their building activity the results would have to be counted as impressive. During the last five years the money spent on church construction in Canada has been about one-quarter of the whole amount spent on school construction; and there are indications that this spending will now increase substantially as many new suburban congregations get their funds and their organization ready for church-building.

It is no small feat for a group of strangers to gather together in their spare time and constitute themselves a permanent institution that can undertake the financial and administrative responsibilities of church-building. Though the suburban church-builders have had advice, moral support, and financial assistance from the parent bodies of their churches, yet they have generally acted on their own initiative. Building the suburban churches has been, historically, the first creative achievement of the new society in the suburbs. A random and heterogeneous collection of families move into their ready-made housing and are soon provided with the ready-made services of stores and schools. Through the early stages of settling down the only bond that ties them together is the formulation of common complaints about their new environment and its incompleteness, about the mud and the lack of play equipment for the children. The transition from this negative and reluctant position into the confidence and optimism of church-building is a truly remarkable process of social maturity. The initiative has generally been carried by young householders who have had practically no experience of managing an undertaking of this kind and who have not previously held a responsible position in a church organization. Observers of the process have commented on the zest with which young suburban church members move into action when they are no longer subdued by the presence of their elders, as in the city's old-established congregations.

Each denomination in a large urban area generally has a Church Extension Committee within its presbyterial or diocesan organization, to aid the process of building new suburban churches. The larger church organizations have sometimes been able to pick out sites in advance when land is being subdivided, by consultation with municipal authorities and with the larger house-building firms. They endeavour to find sites lying well within residential settlements so as to draw their congregations from all directions, recognizing that traffic arteries and industrial lands act as obstructions or boundaries to the area served by a church. Churches look for 2½ or 3 acre sites. Unlike school authorities churches cannot usually buy raw land in advance of subdivision because at this stage the street plan and character of the environment cannot be foreseen. However, commercial builders of family housing are often hospitable to churches so that they can support the claims of their advertising that "churches, schools, and parks have been planned in the project."

They often welcome an opportunity to unload a piece of land which, for one reason or another, is not suitable for house lots—an odd-shaped parcel at a street intersection or adjoining some non-conforming property left behind from previous uses of the land, a quarry or a small industry. Such a site is often turned over to a church for the negative reason that it has no profitable use, rather than because it is positively appropriate for the purpose.

But usually the decision to build a church does not occur until five or ten years after a suburban community has settled in. By this time the choice of possible sites is distinctly limited and decisions have to be made under the pressure of circumstances rather than out of a positive preference for a location. The choices are limited because a church does not easily fit within the typical lot-depth of a residential subdivision and because the usual by-law restrictions on heights and set-backs of buildings make it difficult to place churches on land zoned for residential use. Furthermore, a church attracts a good deal of traffic and, if it is placed within a family neighbourhood, this will be imposed on residential streets. Space must be provided for off-street parking; one car space for each four seats in the church may be required. Whatever may be people's feelings of hospitality towards a church, there is an inevitable intrusion when a traffic-gathering institution is placed within a residential setting. So, in practice, it can be difficult to place a church in the heart of a family neighbourhood where its spire and interesting architectural character might relieve the monotony of standardized housing.

This all points to the advantage of reserving church sites in the development of suburban Town Centres; in this way it would be possible to overcome the difficulties of both timing and site requirements. This subject is discussed here in the context of those parts of Canada that are multi-denominational and not in reference to the homogeneous Catholic communities of Quebec where the church unquestionably takes its place at the heart of the town.

Whatever different shades of doctrine may separate the churches, they are all involved with the same circumstances in the suburbs, and in every denomination the church for family worship has appeared in the same form. In all kinds of architectural variations there is the Sunday School in the basement, the church for grown-ups above, and, in some juxtaposition to these two halls, the office for priest or minister and the kitchen where the ladies of the church put on their aprons and make the lunches and salad suppers which have been the glory of the Canadian churches since frontier days. Each congregation is built around one man and it is the view of most church authorities that four hundred families is a large enough flock for any priest or minister. In a church that has many more than this number the personal contacts between the pastor and his parishioners will suffer or have to be delegated to an assistant. Large churches also tend to multiply their purely recreational and social activities, and the leader of a large congregation is in danger of becoming a secular general manager. This modern preference for a small congregation represents a return to the intimacy of the early Christian meeting-places and an abandonment of soaring ambitions to built great churches of state and authority.

The numerical proportions of Catholic, United Church, Anglican, Presbyterian, Lutheran, and other denominations vary between one region and another in Canada. They also vary in time. There is no assurance that a district which is now predominantly Anglican or Greek Orthodox or Jewish will continue to be so as the population shifts through a century of time. An elementary school is put in the very heart of each family neighbourhood on the confident assumption that families will continue to have children; but there is no assurance that the children are going to be little Anglicans or little Presbyterians. Ethnic factors do have some effect upon the first distribution of city populations, but these factors tend to disappear when the immigrant generation has been absorbed; apart from the language difference which separates English-speaking from French-speaking neighbourhoods it is not in the Canadian tradition to segregate on the basis of ethnic groups or church affiliations. As long as there are a number of separate Protestant churches it is therefore likely that they will draw their congregations somewhat at random from a wide residential territory of mixed population.

In a mixed residential area any single denomination must draw upon two or three contiguous neighbourhoods to form a congregation. There could consequently be a presumption in favour of locating a church in a Town Centre, where it is equally accessible to all its potential church members. In response to the same circumstances, churches would tend to cluster. From the point of view of accessibility the churches have precisely the same reasons as shops and other social institutions for locating in central positions.

Though it has never been a matter of overt and declared policy, the churches have, in fact, generally chosen sites separated from one another. This has been partly a gesture of generosity, to withdraw from the outward appearance of challenging one another in a competitive, side-by-side bid for membership. It has also been an oecumenical mission, recognizing that a broadly scattered distribution of churches might touch the lives of more people. So a United Church group, seeing that an Anglican or Presbyterian church had already appeared in one neighbourhood, might pass it by in order to reach into an area that had no church of any kind. At an earlier stage in our history, in the settlement of the great open spaces of the West, it was this same collaborative mission that brought about the union of Presbyterian and Methodist churches in 1925, to form the United Church. Perhaps a united front in distributing churches into new frontier settlements of the suburbs could inspire a further process of church union. In this way it might indeed be possible to place a church in every neighbourhood.

But this Protestant united front is not likely to come about in the immediate future. And, with so much in common among the churches, perhaps their shades of difference now become more valuable than their similarities. Perhaps it is desirable that they should remain organizationally separate, to offer a variety of choices in religious interpretation and forms of worship. We suffer already from so many influences of uniformity that we may not welcome a synthetic unity of religion. The search for the truth can follow many paths.

There would be both practical and symbolic values in a cluster of community churches at a suburban Town Centre. There would be economy and convenience in sharing the use of indoor and outdoor spaces already provided for community use. Here church congregations would have the free use of traffic arrangements and car-parking space during hours that do not coincide with the peak loads of shopping and other day-time and week-day traffic. This would offer an important economy in land acquisition. There would also be opportunities to share some of the costs of providing indoor space for the secular programmes of the churches. There might well be collaboration in conducting nursery schools and the kindergarten and primary grades of Sunday School. The buildings and special equipment and organization required for Scouts and Guides, for summer camps and for other healthy secular activities, all offer fruitful opportunities for collaboration without any reduction in the independence of the churches in matters of religious faith. As close neighbours in a Town Centre, the churches of different denominations would be able to join together more strongly in the social enterprises that make them such an important part of every suburban community in Canada.

Finally, the symbolic value of putting the churches squarely at the focus of a community's activities does not need any elaboration. A church tucked away in a neighbourhood setting may be a pleasant retreat from the urgent affairs of life; but, in that position, it is hardly likely to assert itself in people's minds and declare its relationship with the business, educational, and public affairs of the town. If the churches have any meaning and any place at all, in the modern suburbanized city, they must claim a position at the heart of every community.

5. A Town Centre Described

IN ALL THE SUBURBS of North America no Town Centre of the kind we are proposing now exists. There are many fine individual buildings, many interesting fragments, the bits and pieces of the place, scattered here and there. But nowhere have the pieces been composed into a whole design. To describe such a place therefore requires an exercise of imagination that must inevitably be coloured by recollections of many places admired and enjoyed, memories of different times and different countries. And indeed why should this not be so? The stream of memory is part of ourselves and, in adapting these recollections imaginatively to our own circumstances, something entirely new and fresh may emerge.

Everyone has a special collection of places fondly recalled. One person may think of the piazza of a Mediterranean town, with the band playing, where the people come out to promenade up and down in the evening light. Another may think of quiet Oxford quadrangles or of the red geraniums tucked around the fountains of a neat town square in Switzerland. You may see a Beergarden under the linden trees on the banks of the Rhine, crowded and buzzing with conversation, or you may have a glimpse of an old gentleman sitting erect on a bench in the Halifax Public Gardens, watching the children feed the ducks. You may see the yard in front of an old church, withdrawn from the bustling traffic of a Latin American city, or you may remember the civic dignity of an old New England country town or the brick-built squares of colonial America, of Maryland and Virginia. The sources of such recollections are wonderfully diverse and all can contribute to the picture of the Town Centre we desire.

The Town Centre of this imagination consists of four quite distinct parts, each in the form of an open space with buildings faced upon it, and each part having a quite different mood and architectural character. They are at slightly different levels, separated by groves of trees and joined by broad walks with a few shallow steps. You can see from one square to another. Traffic is outside with parking areas at a somewhat lower level and there are entries to them at many different points; but none of this is visible when you are inside the Town Centre. Two or three groups of high-rise apartment buildings are visible nearby and, on one side, there might be a wooded hill enclosing the view.

The Town Centre is a place full of people. They go there in cars and buses and on their feet. Some are in a hurry, some are deliberate in their purpose, and some are just strolling. All have closed behind them the doors of home and have come out to meet the world, to buy or sell, to learn or teach, to persuade or seek—or just to contemplate other people doing these things.

The first part of the Town Centre is the Market Square. Since it is a public place, unlike the familiar kind of shopping centre which is the proprietary interest of an investment company and its captive chain-store tenants, this Market Square has recovered some of the colour and diversity of older markets. Here is a delicatessen offering its owner's unique flavours in sausages and delicacies; here a man-and-wife team is able to compete with the impersonal orthodoxy of larger stores because of their individual taste in furniture and fabrics. And in one corner of the square, under coloured awnings, is a busy throng around the farmers' stalls with their fresh fruits and flowers, garden plants and vegetables; some time ago the old downtown farmers' market became inaccessible to the suburban housewife and this reappearance of the farmers in our midst has been much overdue. On another corner of the square, by way of contrast, are three solemn square-cut stone buildings, like modern temples on an acropolis; the straight-faced imperturbability of the branch banks always provides a delightful foil for the colour and frivolity of a market-place.

Under the trees beside the Market Square is a contemporary version of the old-fashioned Victorian bandstand, blossomed into a fantasy of shapes and colours and lights, a composition in "Son et Lumière" as a centre-piece for social gathering. Beside it, in the shade, is a large paved circle on the ground, gaily furnished with café chairs and tables; here buzzing shoppers meet to compare their purchases, old men and women gossip over a cup of tea, and children demand their ice-cream treats. On winter evenings the circle is transformed into a sheet of ice and, with Viennese waltzes oozing from brass instruments on the bandstand, the scene becomes a modern Krieghoff.

The next part of the Town Centre has a different and more serious mood. Sometimes there is a flood-tide of people and sometimes it is quiet and empty like a tidal harbour. On one side the high walls of a theatre auditorium dominate the paved courtyard. On either side of the auditorium there are ways through to the High School campus with views into a series of quadrangles around which the school is built. In contrast with the austere masonry walls of the theatre there are glimpses of bright colours in the decorations of quadrangles and school buildings: a kind of "back-stage" experimental atmosphere for the processes of education. Across the square, on the other side, is a wide sheltering portico of many columns with benches set out on the paving below. Behind this are the tall windows of the Library linked by the portico with a number of other institutions: a small Art Gallery and Exhibit Hall, the Music Centre with its own library and instrument rooms and a small rehearsal theatre. The Meeting House is a separate building, with rooms for conferences, committees, and for conducting the business and keeping the records of many local organizations.

From morning till midnight the tide of people goes in and out of the Square. Exuberant phalanxes of teen-agers surge out and back to their classes with the rhythm of the clock. Each evening the auditorium regularly swallows and then disgorges an audience. Meanwhile a stream of figures, individuals and side-by-side couples, make their way across to the Library colonnade with books and instruments and conversations and private thoughts. Here, on either side of the Square, are the two ways of education: on one side, the regulated processes of learning within the discipline of class-room and curriculum and, on the other side, the individual freedom of personal search and discovery, the exploration of literature, music, and the arts. Getting an education by either method is partly an inward and private affair; but for most people, however brash, however shy, it is also an urgency to find out if you can do it yourself. So the Square becomes a theatre, a place for performance, for mimicry and protest—preferably in a loud voice and strong colours. And for the performance the stage is not just an empty space but is set with fine sculpture placed here and there beside leafy backgrounds of plants and clipped hedges, in a courtyard of stone paving and reflecting water. The skill of the landscape architect, whose formal art we have almost forgotten in this barren age of city sprawl, is essentially an art of the outdoor theatre, providing settings for throngs of people and intimate places for the duets and solo performances.

The third part of the Town Centre is approached up a few steps and through a gateway. This square is surrounded by continuous three-storey buildings with a covered arcaded walk at ground level; it is more compact and enclosed and has an altogether more city-like style. Immediately in front of the gate is a doorway of large and impressive proportions leading into a building of formal appearance, the very scale of the doorway emphasizing the modest size of the individual human figure. This is the entrance to the Council Chamber where the elected representatives of this town community meet to transact local government business; the whole metropolitan region has a central government which assigns to town councils certain responsibilities for local affairs, particularly those concerned with the Town Centre itself. The anteroom to the Council Chamber also leads, on one side, to the Family and Juvenile Court and to the court-room for Boards of Appeal and, on the other side, to the pay offices for local taxation and public utilities. It thus brings together in one place all the functions of local government. The upper floors of the same building are used by branches and agencies of the federal and provincial governments. From time to time everybody comes into this Square.

On either side, in the shelter of the arcaded walk, are the doorways to groups of offices occupied by doctors and dentists, lawyers and insurance agents, all the professional services and sources of personal advice and aid that sustain the continuity of families. The services of pensions, insurance, health, and family support are closely related to the organs of government behind the great doorway on the Square. These relationships are made clearer here than they have usually been in our sprawling, shapeless cities. Government has become a too remote, impersonal, and distant abstraction because the underlying pattern of social and political structure has not been embodied in the forms of cities. Here the town community is made manifest as a microcosm within the larger society of metropolis and nation, and this Square thus declares the mutual responsibilities of the individual and the state.

Finally, the fourth part of the Town Centre does not have such a clear definition. There is a longer approach in the direction of the wooded hillside that has been visible from the other parts of the Town Centre. A broad walk with benches under the trees leads into an open basin of meadowland sloping gently up the hillside to a road that forms a kind of terrace from which one can look into the Town Centre. Above the level of the road the landscape has been left untouched and, half-concealed by the foliage, several churches raise their towers above the tree-tops. They stand apart from one another, informally among the trees and rocks on the hill. Separated from any other kind of city building, each has a different and distinctive architectural character; one has a modest, puritan black-and-white simplicity and another celebrates in joyful colours and unexpected shapes. They have little in common except that each is in its own way devout.

Such is one Town Centre, in the imagination. Its various parts might be put together in an infinite variety of ways depending upon the form of the surrounding suburbs, the arrangement of traffic arteries and parking, and the opportunities provided by the natural landscape. Besides the engineering requirements of traffic and buildings, there are psychological and symbolic requirements in order that suitable impressions may be made upon the minds of those who use the Centre. For you and I as consumers, the market-place is the vortex of our daily routines; as active performers on the stage of life we draw our knowledge and our skills from educational centres. On government and on the organized institutions of society we depend for the security and continuity within which we live. And, finally, removing ourselves from the material apparatus of living and its expression in the Town Centre, we withdraw for purposes of contemplating why we are all here and what is the meaning of this strange span of consciousness between birth and death. Churches are the principal institutions we possess which are dedicated to this kind of contemplation and, however difficult it may be for many to subscribe to their ancient doctrines, they deserve a special place in the arrangement of the city.

HE CHANGING FAMILY HOUSE

he social history of the period since
946 can be read in the fashions and
orms of houses.

28) Post-war economy of space and materials in the 1½-storey house.
29) The three-bedroom ranch-style for the enlarging families of the nineteen-fifties.
30) The split-level, product of oil furnaces and improved building technology.

(31) The half-level entry intended to make
fuller use of the basement and to separate
the activities of children and parents.
(32) The courtyard plan, perhaps the
opening move towards a more sophisticated
and urbane domestic architecture.

32

33

34

IMAGES

The neighbourhood dedicated to the individualism of the family, in the spacious
American style inspired by Frank Lloyd Wright. (Don Mills, Toronto.)
The apartment-house lifted above the landscape, in the urban manner of
rbusier; anonymous social design exalted above individualism. (Sandringham
ments overlooking the Rideau River, Ottawa. Architects, Peter Dickinson
ates.)

THE CHILD'S EXPANDING WORLD

An enclosed courtyard can at first contain the lives of small children, close to home. (35) Mulgrave Park, low-rental public housing project, Halifax, Nova Scotia. (36) Parkwood Terrace, medium-rental private-enterprise project, Burnaby, British Columbia. (Architects: Gale, Harrison, Buzzelle.)

The plan of the suburbs must provide for the later discovery of larger open spaces and for the high-school child who is finally able to detach himself from home and adventure into the suburban town centre. (37) Vincent Massey Park, Ottawa. (38) The way to school, Don Mills, Toronto.

41

THE TENANT FAMILY

Many young families of modest income are not in a financial position to buy a house in the suburbs; they need to conserve their resources and be free to move where there are the best opportunities for employment. Unfortunately private enterprise has not provided enough accommodation suitable for tenant families, who each need a home with its own front door at ground level, rather than an apartment. Some good examples of economical family housing have recently been built by the federal, provincial, and municipal governments in partnerships under the National Housing Act. The illustrations show public low-rental housing in Vancouver (39); Toronto (40); Cornwall, Ontario (41); and Windsor, Ontario (42).

42

43

44

THE OLDER GENERATION

When children have grown up
and left home many people do
not want to remain in family
neighbourhoods, but prefer the
services of apartment-house
living and the freedom from
maintaining a property. They
usually want to be near the
animated focus of a town
centre and, at the same time,
they need space to enjoy an
outdoor life. These requirements of the older generation
should be incorporated in the
designs of suburban Town
Centres. The illustrations show
housing built for old people by
non-profit companies under the
special terms of the National
Housing Act. (43) Kiwanis
Village, West Vancouver,
British Columbia.
(44) Westacres in suburban
Toronto. (45) May Robinson
House, Toronto (Architects:
Jackson, Ypes & Associates).

45

V

SUBURBAN LIVING

1. People and Space

WITH TOWN CENTRES as the fixed points in the suburbs, the surrounding housing and open spaces can be arranged in an intelligible pattern. Some housing can be clustered intensively around the focus while, farther from the centre, houses can be spread loosely in open space. Contrast and variety in ways of life can be reflected in the contrast and variety of buildings and spaces.

We have passed through a phase of city growth in which the suburbs have contained little but single-family houses and the central areas of the city have provided other varieties of accommodation, either by converting older houses or by replacing them with apartment buildings. In the next phase there will be a dispersal of apartments and other forms of rental housing into the suburbs, directed by the same motives that governed the dispersal of family houses. Apartment-dwellers also want more living space, more room to manoeuvre a car, and more trees in the view. Their places of employment and their friends have also moved to the margins of the city. In the dispersed and multi-nucleated city of the future, the suburbs are no longer going to be the special preserve of family life while the central city contains all the non-family households. In its twenty-year plan for the Toronto region (published in January, 1960) the Metropolitan Planning Board estimated that 120,000 apartment units would be built in the period, of which 37,000 would be in the central city, 15,000 in the inner ring of existing suburbs, and 57,000 dispersed into the new outer suburbs. (To this estimate must be added the considerable quantity of rental housing to be built in the extensive suburban areas lying even farther outside the boundaries of the thirteen municipalities that compose Metropolitan Toronto.) In American suburban areas the shift in emphasis has already far exceeded this expectation; in suburban New York almost 50 per cent of all new housing is in the form of apartments and in Los Angeles County apartments exceed single houses in number in the proportion of three to two. This change in the character of the suburbs is due partly to the larger proportion of families living in rental housing, rather than buying their own homes, and partly to a dispersal of non-family households. A complex of economic and social factors makes any forecast unreliable; but perhaps it would be safe to say that, in the coming decades, at least 20 per cent of Canadian suburban housing will be in rental form, some for family use and some for other kinds of households.

With Town Centres as the key pieces in the suburbs, how are apartments and other forms of housing going to fit into the pattern? Here are some general principles:

1. The households most dependent on the commercial and public services in the Town Centre should be closest to it and those least dependent can be farthest removed. The general effect of this principle will be to place single people, old people, and households of lower income nearest to the focus of community services and, on the other hand, to disperse the more self-sufficient family groups and particularly those of higher income.

2. On the assumption that any commercial or public service should be located where it is most accessible to the greatest number of people, it follows that higher-density housing should be closest to the centre. (Neighbourhoods of single-family housing normally contain 20 to 25 persons per acre, suburban areas with an admixture of rental housing have 35 to 50 persons per acre, and intensive developments of apartment buildings may have from 60 to 100 persons per acre.)

3. Systems of public transportation can operate most efficiently, economically, and swiftly when there are points of concentration, such as Town Centres, where passengers are picked up and delivered. The users of public transportation, principally the younger members of the labour force and elderly people, should therefore be housed nearest to the Centre. Car-borne workers and families with car-borne wives can be most detached.

The application of these principles presents a picture of the Centre: a civic space incorporating shops and community buildings, with clusters of apartment buildings behind, their tall shapes giving definition and enclosure to the whole composition. In the expanse of the suburbs this central composition stands out clearly in density and in height. Farther from these points of climax there is a thinning-out to the low-density family housing on large lots.

The pattern has an inevitable logic to it. The middle-class home-owning family is detached in the outer spaces of the suburbs, self-contained and self-reliant, looking in upon itself and inhabiting a completely equipped autonomous dwelling. Such a family is free and centrifugal. But other kinds of households do not enjoy this self-contained completeness and independence. Old people and young people, single people and even childless married couples, cannot live within themselves but must go outside for the social fulfilment of their lives. They are socially and psychologically dependent and rely upon the services and supports and entertainments of a larger society, whether it is for dancing or Bingo, bright lights or medical care. Though their pleasures and points of view may be very different, looking to the future or looking to the past, yet young adults and old adults have this in common: they cannot live in isolation. Non-family households naturally seek attachments to some social cluster or urban nucleus. An apartment house isolated in the outer reaches of the suburbs has a lonely look. For those without a family the sprawling spaces of single-house neighbourhoods have little attraction.

Life in a city must have its measure of both privacy and sociability and these work in opposite ways for people in families and for people without families. For members of a family, sociability is principally inside the house, at the heart of family affairs; outside space is chiefly valuable because it provides an escape into private contemplation— gardening, for instance, is an essentially unsocial occupation. But for people without a family the rooms of a house are quiet and withdrawn and private; they must go outside to find relationships with other people. Consequently unattached people have, in the past, always tended to gravitate towards the centres of cities. Now a successful migration to the suburbs will depend upon attachments to new centres of activity where there is a mingling of individual lives, where there are shops and lights and something to marvel at and something to admire.

Families living in single houses have their own outdoor space, but people living in higher-density housing do not receive their share of open space in the form of private gardens and park-like family neighbourhoods. Clustered around a Town Centre, they have a way of life that is more truly urban in character, since it depends upon public open space shared by many people. Here a smaller proportion of the population is car-borne and open space is needed right on the doorstep of where people live if it is to perform a social function. To a large extent this requirement for social open space can be fulfilled by the Town Square, the Plaza, or Mall at the heart of the Town Centre where some of the bustle and gaiety of city life can be recaptured in the suburbs. This is the forum where old people meet one another and younger people engage in the gregarious affairs of love and life. This kind of formal outdoor space, with its paved surfaces and civic character, should be regarded as part of the architectural design of the Town Centre itself and its clustered multiple housing nearby. It is an inherent part of the living space of a high-density area.

The site of a suburban Town Centre ought to be chosen with an eye for topography so that there may be glimpses into woods and hills and water. The most successful civic compositions have depended upon this relationship between the climax of a community and an insight into the larger universe. The classic example is the Piazza San Marco in Venice, designed so dramatically to catch the view of the sky reflected in the waters of the Lagoon. What would Fredericton, Deep River, or Kingston be without their glimpses across the water? To capture some glimpse of surrounding landscape and waterscape would be a delightful aspect of a suburban Town Centre.

Finally, there is that *rus in urbe* park which is the glory of many great cities, the local version of the Parisian's Bois de Boulogne, the Londoner's St. James Park, the New Yorker's Central Park, and the Boston Common. The new suburbs are desperately barren of this essential element in the composition of the town and are far removed from the handsome parks near the older parts of cities. Where is the contemporary version of Point Pleasant Park beloved of many generations of Haligonians? High Park in Toronto and Stanley Park, Vancouver, have no suburban counterpart. Where is the place for the sunset stroll and family picnic? Perhaps the new Vincent Massey Park in Ottawa is the most successful modern rendering of the landscape park. Here are allusions to the *fête champêtre* and to the nostalgic places of evenings and changing seasons evoked by the romantic painters such as Claude Lorrain and Corot. These wistful landscapes were the inspiration of Capability Brown, who planted the groves and glades that formed such an admirable setting for the English country-house. The scene was recaptured by Frederick Olmsted, the American landscape architect who designed Central Park, New York, placing in the very midst of that great city a landscape of sentiments and memories.

2. Folk Art and Fine Art

SOMETIMES IT HAS SEEMED that the long traditions of domestic architecture have been forever shattered by the brutal forces of mass-production. Can there ever occur again the enduring pleasure that clings to the traditional houses of old England and New England, to the old stone houses of Quebec, and the mariners' cottages of Nova Scotia? Can modern architecture and building technology ever restore what we have lost, except in imitation and mockery? The suburbs are confused by the contradictions of uniformity and restless individualism; it is difficult to find an artistic attitude that reconciles the benefits of standardized production with a lusty striving for personal expression. The stock house in the builders' subdivision bears on its face all the bruises and bandages of this artistic conflict; its simple standard form is plastered with odds and ends of artificial stonework, gimcrack gables, and front doors of tortured ingenuity.

There is an important difference between the art of the single-family house and the art of designing forms of multiple housing. One is an expression of individualism and the other is a social expression. It is the difference between the architectural attitudes of Frank Lloyd Wright and of Le Corbusier. The former expresses the individualism, autonomy, and independence which are the aims of North American family life; the latter expresses the cohesion of a society in which people are interdependent upon one another, projecting their personalities in action with other people, rather than through the display of possessions. A recognition of these differences has a bearing upon the aesthetic criticism of the suburbs. Architectural purists are usually offended by the fads and fashions and follies in the design of small homes in the suburbs and would like to see a more restrained and disciplined order of architecture. They are right, of course, in being highly critical of the deplorable blunders in the architectural proportions and groupings of small houses and in the ill-considered combinations of materials and colours; but it would deny the very nature and *esprit* of family housing if there were a restraint upon the use of current fashions (and even current follies) of design. Perhaps the designing of small houses is a bit nearer to the art of millinery than the art of civic design. Houses must all go through a stage of being "old hat," of showing the follies of the day before yesterday, before they acquire the charm of "period pieces." So, in the maverick spirit of Wright, perhaps we should not be too severe with the egocentricities of family houses. But a quite different aesthetic judgment seems appropriate to the multiple housing that might be clustered around a Town Centre. This is quite properly an exercise in civic design because its purpose is not to express the unique individuality of each household; the aim is to provide for privacy and anonymity within a framework of community organization.

The design of family housing should be regarded as a lively popular art, constantly responsive to new modes of expression, both serious and not so serious. In this respect it is a vernacular or folk art, in the rich vein of Rogers and Hammerstein rather than in the more rarified taste of the avant-garde. A commercial house-builder can respond to these influences through the wit and imagination of a skilful architect. The houses that he builds in any one year may bear the imprint and hallmark of that year's standard production. But each succeeding year may bring fresh, graceful, and surprising responses to new social situations, in new ways of treating the internal and external spaces of a house. These are the genuine sources of variety in the suburbs.

The story of the last dozen years, for instance, can be read on the face of the suburbs and will not be devoid of interest to later generations. The post-war period began with a return to the 1½ storey house with living space on the ground floor and sleeping space within the pitch of the roof; this traditional house, familiar in Quebec, the Maritimes, and New England, is of all architectural forms the most economical in use of house space and building materials. In the late 1940's economy was necessary because of the shortage of building materials and because families had not yet been able to accumulate post-war savings. The limitations of this form of house soon became evident: it is not possible to put three bedrooms and a bathroom within the roof space over a modest living area. By the early 1950's there were two or three children in the post-war family, and it required at least three bedrooms; the sleeping space had to be brought downstairs, as it were, and put beside the living area to form the familiar "ranch" bungalow. A basement for this bungalow required an excavation twice as large as the floor area of a 1½ storey house, but this expense came to seem unnecessary with oil-fuelled, electric-fired furnaces which occupied so little space. (At the same time Father's heroic role in the family, as the essential shoveller of coal, was doomed and he became just a silent TV sitter.) So in the later 1950's the "split-level" introduced a neat trick to fulfil three requirements all at the same time: it saved half the basement excavation, it put only half a flight of stairs between the living floor and the useful clean space in the remaining half of the basement, and it made it possible to put a higher ceiling over the living-room.

Following this transition from 1½ storey to ranch bungalow to split-level there have been at least three new directions in which the design of small houses has moved. The introduction of the so-called "family-room," linked to the kitchen and children's bedroom, has given a new hope to Father, that he may be emancipated and permitted to withdraw to the seclusion of a modest private parlour. Enlargement in the sizes of families has also brought second thoughts about reducing the size of the basement; the "split-level entry," with the front door at ground level and half a flight of stairs either up or down, has thrown a new light into the buried half of the house. And most recently there has been considerable interest in the idea of a courtyard design with the walls of the house enclosing three sides of an outdoor room; this might restore the pleasure in plants and bring outdoor living into a closer and more intimate relationship with the house. It is a move towards a more sophisticated and urbane use of the small house and lot, inspired both by the earliest forms of Mediterranean house and by the Georgian town-house.

It is clear from this record of evolution within the brief span of a dozen years that the products of house-builders are not doomed to monotony. Suburban builders who are willing to pay for the invention of good architects may draw upon an infinite and ever changing variety of designs, without losing the economic advantages of project-scale building. The real curse of monotony is to be seen in the work of those house-builders who fail to progress along this evolutionary path and seek to conceal their inflexibility behind superficial ornaments. Furthermore, very little has yet been done to explore the full range of effects that can be obtained by grouping houses of standard design into all manner of compositions. Turning houses this way and that way, butting them together into rows, using them to enclose landscaped courts with hedges and fences, withdrawing them into little clusters back from the main street— the "unit" family house can be used in an infinite number of compositions. The design of suburban family neighbourhoods could be analogous with the eighteenth-century use of standard forms in music, architecture, and painting: the disciplined, elegant antiphonal exercise of ringing the changes on a small range of melody, proportion, and subject.

The most successful designing of family houses seems to have the freshness and spirited invention of a folk art. Don't let us take the heart out of it by applying standards of artistic judgment that are too solemn and severe. The family neighbourhood is, after all, the land of the nursery and lively youth.

3. The Young and the Old

PEOPLE WHO DON'T LIVE in family groups, both old and young who are particularly dependent on community services, have tended to stay near the old centres of cities where these services have been more easily available. City conditions have tended to separate suburban families from other kinds of household, because there has been a failure to provide in the suburbs the kind of living arrangements that many other people need. This segregation has had a number of disadvantages.

In order to provide for the expanding number of non-family households within the older part of the city there has been a continual process of improvisation. Former neighbourhoods of family housing have been exposed to clumsy acts of conversion, misuse, overcrowding, and other damage; this abuse brings a blight from which there is no recovery and there is a consequent wastage of the community's valuable stock of housing. The centres of all big cities have suffered from this blight of improvisation and the ultimate decline into slum conditions. It has been a lamentable characteristic of the old single-centred city. The new kind of many-focused suburbanized city could offer a release from this problem, if all kinds of households could take their places near to Town Centres.

While the centre of the city has suffered from an oversupply of non-family people, the suburbs have suffered from an undersupply. They have not been there to help pay the taxes with which to build the schools and all the other public requirements on the growing margins of the city. They have been cut off from normal social relationships with the new cycle of life in the suburbs; the loss has been mutual.

We may now look forward to an increasing dispersal of non-family housing so that future suburbs may contain a fairly complete cross-section of the whole urban population, which consists of the following principal elements:

A. FAMILY HOUSEHOLDS
    1. Young families,
        the head of the family under 35 years   about 21 per cent
    2. Middle-period families,
        the head of the family 35 to 65 years   54 per cent
    3. Older families,
        the head of the family over 65 years   12 per cent

B. NON-FAMILY HOUSEHOLDS (households that are not based
        on a married couple or on a parent-child
        relationship)
    1. Young people, under 35 years   2 per cent
    2. Middle-aged people, 35 to 65 years   6 per cent
    3. Older people, over 65 years   5 per cent
    Note: In this B Group about two-thirds are single people living alone and
about one-third are single people living in groups of two or more people.

Five or six years after marriage a family is first drawn into an Elementary School neighbourhood; at this stage the family income has not yet reached its full capacity to buy housing space and a two-bedroom unit may be space enough. But the largest amount of housing has to be built to the requirements of the middle period of life when the greatest amount of space is needed for growing families. The amount of house-space and the whole form and substance of family neighbourhoods are determined by the economic capacity of families in this middle period. It is a thirty-year span of life, which may reach its conclusion in three more or less simultaneous events: when the youngest child of the family graduates from school, when the householder's income steps down from employment earnings to the more modest level of a pension, and when the mortgage payments on the house have been completed. The average owner of a house financed in 1961 under the National Housing Act was 34 years of age and had either one or two children. His annual income was $5,810 and the house he built or bought cost him $14,474. The new owner made a down-payment of $2,475 and undertook monthly payments of $105 against principal and interest on the mortgage and on municipal taxes. Average monthly payments represented 21.7 per cent of his income. Few families are ready to embark on this enterprise before their income has reached $4,000 a year and the majority of purchasers are in the $4,000 to $6,000 income range. This means that between 30 and 40 per cent of families in cities have not graduated to an income level that would enable them to buy a new N.H.A. home in the suburbs. Some are on the way to making the grade and some never do.

In the last few years there has been a tendency to enter upon home-ownership before the middle period of life; about a quarter of all N.H.A. house-purchasers have been in the 25-to-30 age group and another quarter in the 30-to-35 age group. The houses built to match their incomes have necessarily been smaller and cheaper than the houses they might have been able to afford somewhat later in life. This has affected the whole quality of the housing stock passed on to succeeding generations in our cities. In order to improve the quality and size of family houses it may, indeed, be wise to discourage young families from purchasing new houses and give greater emphasis to the upgrading of families in the middle period of life. This would be possible if there were a larger supply of suburban rental housing for young families.

Most families make three or four moves within the middle period because of changes in income, family size, and place of employment. (In recent years more than one-quarter of all families receiving family allowances have moved within a year.) The advance-guard in this turnover of houses has been able to accomplish these shifts as their equity in home-ownership continually increases and can be used as down-payment on successively more expensive new houses. The system has not worked smoothly, however, because of the difficulty of refinancing used houses in the interests of those in the lower-income echelons of the housing turnover. Changes in the National Housing Act, to support the refinancing of used houses, could remedy this defect in the market and aid the turnover of houses in family neighbourhoods.

The cycle of life has a symmetry: on either side of this middle period is a phase of married life when a man and wife are inclined to be foot-loose and need a housing arrangement of minimum commitment. Many of the young families (21 per cent of all households) and the older families (12 per cent) have no compulsion to live in neighbourhoods organized around elementary schools and are not aided by the whole system of mortgaged home-ownership.

Young married couples need to be flexible in their adjustment to employment opportunities, able to move from one city to another or from one district to another. Until the wage-earner's career has taken shape and started him on the income ladder, he must resist the alluring propaganda of home-ownership. At first he and his wife are probably both workers, leaving their apartment empty all day. They are the natural cliff-dwellers in high-rise apartments because they do not need their own day-time open space. For them, outdoor space is the night-time horizon of the city, the sky, and the bright lights to be seen from windows and balcony. Then their housing requirements change abruptly and radically on the arrival of the first child. The ground in daylight sun and shadow suddenly comes into close-up view: a place to sit out-side, a barricaded infant play-space, and a route to walk on a paved surface to the stores and social destinations in the Town Centre. Now they must move from high-rise to horizontal living space. The architec-ture of the suburbs should be able to express these changes and con-trasts in the passage of life.

Older married couples, when they are released from the responsibilities of raising a family, have some of the same needs as young married couples. It is another period of adjustment and minimum commitment when new choices have to be made in the location and way of life. Though a beneficent State has protected old age, with measures for health and security of income, yet Canadian cities are still at a primitive stage in providing a congenial living environment for this part of our lives. Too many retired couples have been driven to take refuge in the southern United States, not so much in pursuit of a more hospitable climate, but to escape from unwelcome imprisonment in dark rooming-houses and second-rate apartments on the fringes of downtown. Old people have been associated in the public mind with old housing and there is a popular mythology that every generation of grandparents will happily return to old haunts in the centre of the city. Let us realize that the next wave of old people will have spent their lives in the suburbs and have few sentimental ties with central city streets.

About 1¼ million people in Canada are over the age of 65, and 54 per cent of them live at home in the company of wives, husbands, and chil-dren. Another 16 per cent continue to maintain a home of their own, either living there alone or having the company of someone who is not a member of the family. The remaining 30 per cent of the whole over-65 group have made some quite fundamental change in their living arrange-ments. More than half of them (17 per cent of the whole group) have gone to live with relatives, usually with sisters and other family connec-tions rather than with their own children. A smaller number, about 8 per cent, are living in the homes of people not related to them and, finally, about 4 per cent have taken refuge in some kind of institution for the sick or the aged. (These figures are taken from the 1951 Census; at the time of writing, the 1961 Census figures are not available. It will be interesting to see how these circumstances have changed in a decade.)

In this period of life the situation is more difficult for women than for men, partly because women commonly marry husbands older than themselves and consequently survive their husbands through a longer period of old age, and partly because women tend to live longer. While 65 per cent of elderly widowers continue to live in their own family households, women face a longer span of life separated from home and family. Only 46 per cent in the over-65 group are still living at home with their families and more women than men find themselves seeking shelter in the homes of relatives (22 per cent compared with 12 per cent). In Canada about 72,000 women over 65 live alone.

Evidently the dangers of the "mother-in-law problem" have been taken to heart. About 20,000 women over 65 are living in their children's homes but six times as many have elected to avoid the difficulties of this situation and have gone to live with other relatives. It is noticeable that Ontario families are the most hospitable to mothers-in-law. And contrary to the general impression that Quebec is the traditional setting of the patriarchal family, the record shows that Ontario has a considerably larger proportion of households containing three generations, from grandparents to grandchildren.

The benign patriarchal figure in the three-generation family, held in awe for his sagacity and experience, has been almost wiped out by the migration to the big city. We have tried to restore dignity to this passage of life by providing financial independence so that old age can be entered, not with apprehension, but with a confidence that it is a destination to be sought and enjoyed. To find a suitable place to live is the first concern of old age, a problem too often still treated with apologetic and patronizing references to "senior citizen" and "the sunset."

The strongest motive in planning housing for older people should be to preserve intact the personal contacts and associations that have been the fabric of their lives. Independence and freedom are sustained longest in a familiar setting where personality is accepted and respected among neighbours. Sickness, loneliness, and all the attendant psychosomatic infirmities are not so likely to reach lethal dimensions amid familiar surroundings and the normal scenes of active life. Placed on the threshold of a Town Centre old people would be able to reach out in three directions. They could visit nearby family neighbourhoods where there may be children, grandchildren, and other personal connections. They could quickly reach churches, libraries, shops, and medical advice within the Centre itself. And they could penetrate into the open landscape of the park.

More than any other members of the community, old people have suffered from the scatter and confusion of the suburbs. They have been cut off from society because of the new space-time dimension and the assumptions of ubiquitous mobility. A new focus of community services and an easy walking access to the centre of local affairs would be a merciful gesture to ourselves, the old people of the future.

VI

THE OLD CENTRE OF THE CITY

WHAT IS TO HAPPEN at the old centre of the city is, to some extent, the obverse of what is to happen in the suburbs. What is to be taken away and what is to be left? As the central business district assumes the function of a management centre for the Regional City, new demands are placed upon the older residential areas that surround the centre; shifts of population and improvements in standards of living bring changes and uncertainties to this part of the city. Much of the stock of housing that has accumulated there through the last century is no longer relevant to the new role of the city centre. Much of it is too old fashioned, inconvenient, and deteriorated to serve any useful purpose except as a refuge for low-income families and for old people who cannot find suitable housing elsewhere.

The central areas of most North American cities have entered a period of obsolescence and deterioration and all attempts to take a long-term view of the prospects have led to alarming conclusions. In the United States a "conservative estimate" has shown a need for the replacement of nearly seven million substandard dwelling units and the rehabilitation of another two million at a cost of approximately 125 billion dollars. Though Canadian cities have not inherited the same massive slum areas, because we did not share in the early build-up of a large, low-paid industrial labour force, yet the quantity of obsolete housing is on a considerable scale. In its 1955 report on *Housing and Social Capital* the Gordon Commission commented that by 1980 about one million units in Canada would be more than seventy-five years old ("by North

American standards a distinctly advanced age") and concluded that a replacement of 330,000 units would be a conservative estimate of the requirements.

The sheer magnitude of the task has had a withering effect upon political initiative, and even the protagonists of the public housing movement have wilted. Will cities be chained to a never ending sequence of removing obsolete housing and putting back new housing at public expense? Will the old centres of cities be encased with an ever enlarging monolithic territory of public housing, sheltering a subsidized population? The costs of acquiring slum land for the Regent Park South project in Toronto and for the Jeanne Mance project in Montreal were alarming: $176,000 an acre for the former and $340,000 an acre for the latter. The very fact that the land was so expensive seemed to impose an obligation to use the space to maximum capacity; so high-rise housing was built, a form of structure that extends still further the public costs of housing low-income families. What could be the future of this perplexing chain of events?

A new illumination was shed upon this teasing problem when it was perceived that the rebirth of central city areas was indeed much more than just a housing operation. The healthy condition of what surrounds the city centre depends upon the health of the "core" itself. The first North American cities to make this discovery were Pittsburgh and Philadelphia. The cleaning-out of Pittsburgh's heartland and the building of the "Golden Triangle," the shining new centre of the city, shed an entirely new light on what had seemed to be the arid duties of urban redevelopment. This discovery was new to North America but was a fulfilment of what had long been known to European architects and planners. Le Corbusier and the advance-guard of European designers were the first to rediscover the "core." They knew that ever since city people had first gathered in the Athenian agora and Roman forum, in the Italian piazza and Cathedral square, this emphasis on a central place had been the tradition of Western cities. The theme had appeared in Le Corbusier's first visions of rebuilt Paris, in the new image of a radiant city of skyscrapers and parks. The Pennsylvania cities of Pittsburgh and Philadelphia were the first in North America to recover this old and ever new tradition.

Both cities had been cursed with dreary and disinterested business centres, the tired countenances of cities that had grown wealthy in the railroad age. Beneath this grimy surface Philadelphia rediscovered its own rich and honourable history, the old colonial city of charming brick houses. A space was cleared about Independence Hall and a garden

planted there. The brutal, grime-gathering "Chinese wall" of the railway yards was removed, and a new centre of civilization carved out of
the nineteenth-century confusion. Trees now grow again in the city
squares and people can walk to admire the reborn city they are creating.
Most remarkable is the return of families to live in the old town houses
on the Georgian streets near the city centre. Like Georgetown in Washington, this neighbourhood of modest brick terraces, with shuttered windows and walled gardens, is restored to family use.

Following the examples of Pittsburgh and Philadelphia a number of
other American cities, notably Detroit, Baltimore, Chicago, and Washington, are engaged in renewing their central areas on a heroic scale.
Men of imagination have reoriented the rather reluctant and desultory
programmes of slum-clearance into a major renaissance of the hearts of
these lively cities. To resurrect historic buildings out of the crowded
wreckage and blight, to rediscover the pleasures of city squares retrieved
from traffic, to capture a sense of history in building new architecture
amid the old—these are the ancient and modern enjoyments of city life.
The core of the city is one indivisible composition. Restoration, then, is
not just a matter of clearing some slums here, solving some traffic problems there, replacing some obsolete office blocks.

The revival of these city centres during the last decade has given a
new vitality to city planning because it has shown once again the importance of the heartland places that are the energy centres of every urban
community, large or small, central or suburban. These are the permanent
places that must survive all the fleeting transformations of a lifetime.
The experiences of Philadelphia and Pittsburgh also remind us that
people are not just the victims of circumstances but have a surprising
opportunity to change the most rigid and conventional features of their
environment, if they have a sufficiently strong image of what they want
and the ability to organize for its achievement. The stories of Pittsburgh's
and Philadelphia's renaissance are now part of the saga of American
democracy.

In Canada a similar reorientation must occur. Before the 1949 legislation for public housing had produced more than a handful of minor
projects, new federal government offers were made so that sites from
which slums had been removed could be used for purposes other than
public housing. The 1954 version of the National Housing Act enables
the federal government to join with a city, sharing the costs equally, in
clearing obsolete housing and disposing of the sites for whatever purposes may best fulfil the needs of the community. Without this change
we would still be faced with the alarming prospect of an ever enlarging

enclave of public housing surrounding the central cores of cities as successive rings of old housing fall into decay and have to be replaced. Under present arrangements in the National Housing Act the city of Halifax, Nova Scotia, has already cleared central slums so that the land can be used for commercial purposes and has built the Mulgrave Park housing project some distance from the city's centre to receive displaced families. Of course it will continue to be necessary to use some central land for low-rental housing because some of the employment opportunities for low-income workers still occur near the central core of the city. But even the excellent architecture of the Regent Park South project in Toronto and the Jeanne Mance project in Montreal could not conceal the obvious limitations imposed upon family life by the high-density conditions of central area housing. In its twenty-year plan the Toronto Metropolitan Planning Board has proposed that 25,000 low-rental units should be built in the metropolitan area of which only 7,500 would be in the form of direct replacements in the central area; 1,500 units would be built in the existing inner suburbs and 16,000 units would be placed in the outer suburbs to be developed in the coming two decades. It is proposed that, of this whole number, from 15,000 to 20,000 units would be for families and about 7,500 for old people. All of this housing on suburban sites will have to be closely related to public transportation and to community services and so become an important part of suburban Town Centre planning.

Meanwhile the big cities are beginning to exert themselves to give new vitality to their central cores. In Montreal, the Place Ville Marie and other vast projects in the vicinity of Dominion Square and Dorchester Street will give a new face and new mood to this metropolitan heart. The Civic Square and new City Hall of Toronto will give a strong focus that the city has never possessed since the railway was so callously allowed to cut off the heartland of the city from its natural water-front site. (For a city to deny itself such a prospect over the Bay to the crescent of islands was one of the historic acts of civic renunciation; for here was an ideal relationship between a city centre and an open waterscape and landscape.) In the National Capital Commission's most recent plans for the central area of Ottawa the core of the city receives a new concentration with pedestrian spaces enclosed by groups of buildings. Winnipeg's and Windsor's plans for urban renewal embody open spaces and groups of civc and commercial buildings to give new dramatic value to the core. The theme continually asserts itself. Having put a new heart into the central city it will then be possible to elevate the whole character of the surrounding residential areas. The most substantial improvement to be made will be the restoration of open space of all kinds, green park-space and hard-surface traffic-space; for it is the pursuit of space that has taken city people out into the suburbs and accelerated the decline of housing in central areas. Large tracts of family housing in the older inner suburbs can be kept in active use only if these neighbourhoods can be made comparable with the new outer suburbs, in the safety of their streets, in the enjoyment of green spaces, and in the removal of business and industry that has been allowed to intrude. These would be the most rewarding aims of public expenditure in the declining areas of cities.

Just as the first approach to urban redevelopment seemed to foreshadow an infinity of public housing in the place of slums, so the whole apparatus for producing the suburbs seemed at first to contemplate nothing but an infinity of single-family houses. Our appreciation of the problems has changed. The generator of urban renewal has turned out to be the revival of the heartland of the city and, in the suburbs, there is a corresponding need for emphasis on Town Centres.

VII

THE END IS EXCELLENCE

THIS EXPLORATION STARTED OUT as a quest for the missing piece in the suburbs, in response to the laments over confusion and monotony and pointlessness. The search led to an examination of cities, their changing nature, and the unfolding ideas of what they might be. We hoped to discover the talisman.

The quest started with a purpose specific to the suburbs, but has led to all kinds of questions about cities in general and about Canadian cities in particular. At the end of the path is the ultimate question: the question of excellence. Is it possible for the present kind of North American city to flower into something really excellent, that would lift people's hearts and would make our children rejoice in their generation? Where could this occur in the spread-out regional city? What form could it take? How could it happen? These must be the end questions if we can believe that cities are the culminating achievements of civilization, the repository of the intellectual arts. In this context, excellence is not just the ultimate efficiency that we may some day expect from motor cars and the whole network of expressways and traffic engineering. Nor does it refer to the majestic size and glistening efficiency of the great steel-and-glass office buildings now rising in business centres. Nor does it mean the passing fashions and delights of individual houses, rich with decorative allusions and whims. No, ultimate excellence in the city has to appear where the hearts and spirits and minds of its people are touched. The most intense and eager search for expression can only take place, as it were, on tiptoe: by a stretching-out to find what is just beyond reach and understanding. Brunelleschi's and Michelangelo's domes were not made like bridges, to get to the other side. They were set high above the ground in a prodigious gesture of wonder and worship.

People of other ages have been able to give their excellent and best work to the building of cities. To marvel at these masterpieces North Americans often leave their uninspiring suburbs and, as tourists, travel to distant places. Are we to believe that every conceivable possession is going to be given to our affluent society, but that this final prize will always elude us? Perhaps, like most rich people, we are fat and lazy and can only bask in our own expensive vulgarity. Perhaps reaching pinnacles is not important to us when it is so comfortable in the valleys. Anyway, it may be said, excellence is out of date; the beauties of the classical, mediaeval, and baroque cities could not have a modern counterpart because we are no longer naive enough to waste our substance on building temples, cathedrals, and useless monuments. Those were the arts of an earth-bound age and we are off into space.

Indeed, it certainly seems that excellence is a very difficult accomplishment in an age of mass-production to serve a market of average people. Excellence has been chopped off at the top end just as poverty has been removed at the bottom. This is the sacrifice society has had to make for democracy. There is left only a middle, mild, bland product that neither stimulates nor nauseates: an innocuous city full of regulation buildings filled with conforming furniture for the use of orthodox people. Sometimes even poverty may seem more acceptable than these bland comforts. The fisherman's cottage on the storm-swept rocks of Nova Scotia, the Eskimo's igloo, and the settler's log cabin have a simple authority that cannot be matched in the lush meadows of suburbia. There was a warmth of comfort and security in Mrs. Moody's log cabin in the bush, whose flickering light in the windows was scarcely visible through the dark trees; but the dream has been tarnished in its realization. Even the friendly, charming confusion of early Canadian towns has been replaced by the stereotyped sanitary housing of the modern city. Yes, civic improvement has not often been touched by the magic hand of the artist.

There is another way of looking at this democratic middle-of-the-road standard of design, a plausible claim for the true attribute of excellence. The real art of today, it may be said, is in this very act of contriving and smoothing and compromising. *Ars celare artem.* Here is the brilliant synthesis, the version that satisfies the committee because it really has no expression, no meaning at all. There is no doubt that the highest and most expensive skills are dedicated to this art of anonymity and many important works of contemporary art and architecture are of this kind; the new steel-and-glass office structures in our big cities continue to pile up into the sky, cold and unemotional in their architectural purity. They express nothing more than the cubic feet of efficient and refined working space, because there is nothing else for them to express. In Montreal these latest giants bear the names of banks, in Toronto they are the trade-marks of oil and insurance, while on Park Avenue, New York, the glistening new packages bear the brand-names of whiskey and soap. These are all admirable works of architectural engineering but any artistic quality they possess is of a cold and compromising kind. It is an art that belongs with highway engineering: the cars travel up and down an elevator shaft instead of horizontally on a street. It is a sterilized and antiseptic way of building the centre of the city, in tune with the industrial design of automobiles and the white goods in the kitchen.

Then there is the contrary view that the only remaining opportunity for vigorous and inspired art is in the expression of protest and anger. The sensitive person must rebel against the system and the establishment; he must be an angry young man, the leaning figure with the beard, the listless arms, and the cigarette. In the shadows of noncommitment he rejects both the daylight and the bright lights. He belongs neither to the left nor to the right, hostile to both the great systems that dominate the world, for both communism and Americanism seem to demand slavish conformity. A plague upon both your houses! Better to withdraw to that middle world of Europe, to the pubs of London or to the Costa Brava, than to be swallowed up by either system! Indeed one could not expect to understand a great deal of modern painting and contemporary writing without sympathy for this mood of angry protest. For this must always be the emotional source of art, the passionate seeking of man for individuality amidst the crowd: the contest of the few against the many. It is at the very heart of the artistic, social, and intellectual problem of building cities: how to sustain the individual against the tyrannies of the multitude.

Are we to lose from our cities all that is exceptional and excellent, in preference for the democratic goal of the universally acceptable? Is the art of city-building to be just the unimpassioned synthesis of what is regulated, scheduled, and zoned to an inoffensive normality? The terms "to excel" and "to conform" are clearly contradictory. The angry young man is right in protesting that only those who can stand outside the system are capable of true artistic expression. But is the artist who thus questions the validity of the system to be rejected as an alien speaking a language of protest no one understands? What about the saints and martyrs whose memory we hallow?

These questions have not appeared to be relevant to the practical tasks of building cities and suburbs; with the consequence that the practical engineering approach has effectively blotted out any opportunities for excellence in the modern city. The omission must be repaired by deliberate action to enshrine this purpose—excellence—at the very centre of the places where we live. This is the real intention of the proposal that has here taken shape in the idea of the suburban Town Centre. If the artist and the critic, the searching sculptor and angry young man, the questioner and Utopian can find no place here, then there is no place for them in town.

The Town Centre, as an idea, is not intended to provide a doctrinaire, geometrical solution to all the problems of planning communities. It may assume an infinite variety of form and content and symbolism in giving expression to central purposes and questions around which our lives revolve. We know very well that our lives do not revolve round the steel and glass skyscrapers at the centre of the city, nor around the new shopping centres in the suburbs; these are part of the efficient, systematic commercialized city but they are not concerned with the meaning of life itself, with learning and thinking and contemplating and confronting people with questions. So they can have neither true artistic expression nor true excellence. Their neutrality, anonymity, and conformism are part of the service.

A stranger observing us in our suburbs might conclude that North Americans had been utterly subdued into conformity by the great corporate systems of democracy and industry. Yet in fact this is not the truth; the suburbs give a false impression of what is in our minds. We have simply failed to give expression to the motives and purposes that govern us; in the arranging of cities we have been inarticulate. As a matter of fact Canadians and Americans are inclined to be both inquisitive and doubting and are great seekers after the truth.

There is the philosophical quest, the pursuit of knowledge about the physical and spiritual world in which we live. This is the aim of education and of learning in science, religion, and the contemplative arts. Schools and libraries and churches and other places where this purpose can be pursued clearly have a first place at the centre of our towns. Whether a person tries to penetrate the unknown through economics or painting or religion or literature, he is engaged on the same ultimate endeavour. There ought to be places for this purpose, near at hand for everyone, and in a variety of choices.

Then there is the social purpose to be pursued in the many different ways in which people confront one another, with questions and assertions. There are the casual, unexpected, and lingering meetings in the market-place and town square which had always supplied the civilized graces of city life until the car intruded upon our lives: the Champs Elysées and Hyde Park Corner: leaning over the bridge, lingering on the steps, or sitting on the benches under the elms. There are also the more formal social arrangements offered by indoor and outdoor sports, in auditoriums, and in recreation and performance of all kinds. Cities can be designed to invite these civilized relationships.

"Cities can be designed. . . ." Can they?

The problem is, of course, that the suburbs are not made by the people who live there. They arrive afterwards. Suburbanites have had cause for complaint that what they find on arrival is not an expression of their desires and ambitions. The suburbs don't look remotely like anything they could have imagined; this has not been the fulfilment of a dream. To a large extent the suburbs have been an accident, the consequence of an elaborate interplay of forces in land speculation, in traffic arrangements, and in the bid for consumer markets. The people who arrive in the suburbs have been inarticulate; they have neither formulated nor expressed their desires. How could they? They weren't there when the decisions had to be made. The settlers on the modern frontier are not like the early pioneers who cleared the chosen land themselves, selected the site for the homestead, and made their own environment. Making the suburbs has been a complex, impersonal, greedy, industrial process for converting raw land into a finished salable product, housing and commercial services.

There must be an institutional embodiment of the future "we" who come to live in the suburbs, a form of public Trustee to represent the interests of the future residents while the suburbs are in the making. This must be a public body with powers to buy the community land, to make plans for each Town Centre, and to start developing its buildings and open spaces. When the Centre has grown to a mature stage and when the surrounding community has settled down and solidified, then the Trustee organization has discharged its responsibilities and can surrender the Town Centre property to the established local government. Here, indeed, the fine art of politics must take its place in building the new kind of suburbanized city, the *polis* in its modern form. The whole static structure of local government must be given a new flexibility and fresh face to deal with this lusty, long-legged growth of cities.

The building of a city is an enterprise in which public and private interests are in partnership. In the rapid growth of the suburbs the forces of private enterprise have become formidable and energetic; they need to be matched in the partnership with an equally strong form of public agency to fight the battles for those who are not yet there. In fact, if any kind of order is to be made in the suburbs, the public agency must be first in the field to supply the focal centre that should largely determine the disposition of what is to be built by private developers. Unfortunately, local governments have possessed no recognized agency to perform this role and there has been little coherent action by the municipal bodies which eventually have to develop suburban property: the school boards, parks boards, library boards, and recreation agencies. The strength of local government has been divided and fragmented. This departmentalization is undoubtedly necessary during the period of continuing management but is a weakness at the initial stage of city-building, in the face of the powerful concentrations of strength for developing housing and shopping centres.

The proposal for suburban Town Centres embodies the principle of Trusteeship for the paramount interests of the future community. The Centre is seen as an island of community land surrounded by the expanse of private residential property in the suburbs. The community land is held in public ownership, its design and development under the direct control of the Trustee organization, and it is assigned in three ways: (1) some land for public use for education, recreation, and the enjoyment of open space; (2) some on long-term leases to community institutions such as churches, and organizations concerned with the public welfare; (3) and some on leases of somewhat shorter duration for business and commercial uses, this reverting eventually to the public domain.

In other ages the central places of cities, the excellent places that dramatized and symbolized the philosophy and purpose of their time, were made by the great institutions of Church and State. These central places took shape gradually through the centuries as populations slowly grew and civilizations flowered. It was a slow process—breaking the stones to build the great temples, cathedrals, and palaces—and the population did not multiply quickly, being threatened by pestilence, ill-health, and war. What a contrast with today's situation! Our population spreads like wildfire, its health carefully protected from the cradle to the grave. We must build a new city every year, every month, every week;

in Canada there are more than a million new houses to be built in the suburbs every decade and, in the United States, a dozen times that number. Time presses upon our heels and we've become accustomed to working in a hurry, accepting the mass-produced, second-rate job in the expectation that it might be done more carefully the next time round. There hasn't yet been time to devise our own instruments of state for building new cities in the suburbs.

New adventures in city-building await us. We may again find out how to make excellent places to be remembered with warm affection. We may discover new and vivid expression of the purposes of life, the pursuit of knowledge, and the confrontation of friends and strangers. But these adventures will come only to those who are bold enough to devise new political processes to achieve those ends, in a way that fits our time and place. This is the essential creative art of local politics: to nurture each new community through its period of growth and finally launch it upon the experience of self-government. This is the central creative act in the politics, the planning, and the architecture of the suburbs.